To G

Through the year with
WORDS OF COMFORT

God Bless you.

Daniel P. Cronin

Through the year with
WORDS OF COMFORT

Compiled by Daniel P. Cronin

ST PAULS

ST PAULS
Middlegreen, Slough SL3 6BT, United Kingdom
Moyglare Road, Maynooth, Co. Kildare, Ireland

© St Paul Publications (ST PAULS) 1990

First published 1990. Reprinted 1994

ISBN 085439 344 7

Printed by The Guernsey Press Co. Ltd, Guernsey, C.I.

ST PAULS is an activity of the priests and brothers of the
Society of St Paul who proclaim the Gospel through the
media of social communication

Contents

Dedicated to my mother
Elizabeth Margaret Cronin

Introduction

The only way to read a collection such as this without being bored is to open it at random and, having found something that interests you, close the book and meditate.

It may well be wise to try to be disciplined and read just one or two days at a time rather than plough through the book from cover to cover in one sitting. Ultimately there are no rules about *Words of Comfort* – just use it in any way you find to be helpful for you. However, allow me to share the thoughts of one of our great spiritual masters, Jean-Pierre de Caussade:

"... employ more of your time in reading good books, and in order to make this more efficacious, set about it in this way:

Begin by placing yourself in the presence of God and by begging his help.

Read quietly, slowly, word for word, to enter into the subject more with the heart than with the mind.

At the end of each paragraph that contains a complete meaning, stop for the time it would take you to recite an 'Our Father', or even a little longer, to assimilate what you have read, or to rest and remain peacefully before God.

Should this peace and rest last for a longer time, it will be all the better; but when you feel that your mind wanders, resume your reading, and continue thus, frequently renewing these same pauses.

Nothing need prevent you from continuing the same method, if you find it useful to your soul, during the time you have fixed for meditation."

That other very quotable person, Ralph Waldo Emerson said with much wisdom:

"'Tis the good reader that makes the good book; in every book he finds passages which seem confidences or asides hidden from all else and unmistakably meant for his ear; the profit of books is according to the sensibility of the reader; the profoundest thought or passion sleeps as in a mine, until it is discovered by an equal mind and heart."

I hope that you will dig deep into this quarry of thoughts and find many things which will bring you solace and healing as you journey through life. It is my privilege to join you on that pilgrimage and very humbly provide one or two signposts which might be useful along the way.

I would like to thank all who have helped in compiling this book and most specially my *Universe* readers, some of whom are published for the first time in this work: viz. Bernard Boon, David Brown, June Chantry, Patricia Davis, Winifred Eddison, Connie Ford, Robina Knewstub and Patricia Vardigans. To Phil Redeyoff and Tom Murphy of Gabriel Communications for their ready collaboration, and finally to Mrs Jennifer Cornish for her contribution in proof reading the text and for many pertinent comments.

If you come across any inspiring thoughts, prayers or quotations which you would like to forward for consideration and possible inclusion in a future volume, please address them to:

Fr Daniel Cronin
"Words of Comfort Book"
Cathedral Clergy House
42 Francis Street
Westminster
London SW1P 1QW

January

1

We fully appreciate that whatever we have done, achieved or acquired in the past is the outcome of your kindness and love, and we earnestly pray, all-wise Lord, that you continue to be with us along life's journey and show us the correct path to follow. Grant us the necessary power and strength of body, mind and spirit to overcome any obstacles on the way.

Zoroastrian

2 Abandonment

What is an abandonment experience?
Is it a leaving oneself on God's doorstep,
    walking into the rest of life,
        not allowing anxiety,
            fear,
            frustration to enter into one?
Is it expecting God to keep one warm,
            secure,
            and safe,
            unharmed?
Is that abandonment ?

Abandonment has nothing to do with warmth of
            womb or arms
            or close clasped hearts.

It is not something done by a child.
It is done to him
It cannot be done to an adult.
It is done by him.
Abandonment is committed only with and in the
    maturity of Christ Jesus.
It is not just a hanging loose.

It is a letting go.
It is a severing of the strings by which one
   manipulates,
   controls,
   administrates
   the forces in one's life.
Abandonment is receiving all things the way
   one receives
   a gift
   with opened hands,
   an opened heart.

Abandonment to God
is the climactic point in any man's life.

Anon.

3 | Abandonment

When, in all our actions, we look upon ourselves as instruments in the hands of God to work out his hallowed designs, we shall act quietly, without anxiety, without hurry, without uneasiness about the future, without troubling about the past, giving ourselves up to the fatherly providence of God and relying more on him than on all possible human means.

In this way we shall always be at peace, and God will infallibly turn everything to our good, whether temporal or eternal.

Jean-Pierre de Caussade 1675 - 1751

Adoration

Set apart a certain amount of time morning and evening, whether the mind be filled with God or not, doing so with no other object than the adoration which is the duty of his creature. Adore him with all the capacity you have, yet without anxiety as to the degree of your success or of your love, as to whether you are concentrated on God or on yourself, whether your time is profitable or wasted ... There is no question here of stages of prayer. We are concerned only with adoring God without any motive save that we are bound in this to accept failure with patience and humility...The value of our prayer depends on the degree to which we die to self in offering it. There is no place for calculations or precautions. Strive to adore and let that suffice.

Jacques Bossuet 1627 - 1704

4 | Ambition

True ambition is a deep desire to live usefully and walk humbly in the grace of God. *Anon.*

5 | Attitudes

THE SMALL BEATITUDES

Blessed are those who can laugh at themselves;
they will have no end of fun.

Blessed are those who can tell a mountain from a
  molehill;
they will be saved a lot of bother.

Blessed are those who know how to relax without
  looking for excuses;
they are on the way to becoming wise.

Blessed are those who are sane enough not to
  take themselves too seriously;
they will be valued most by those about them.

11

Happy are you if you can take small things seriously
    and face serious things calmly;
you will go far in life.

Happy are you if you can appreciate a smile and
    forget a frown;
you will walk on the sunny side of the street.

Happy are you if you can be kind in understanding
    the attitudes of others even when the signs are
    unfavourable;
you may be taken for a fool but this is the price of
    charity.

Blessed are those who think before acting and pray
    before thinking;
they will avoid many blunders.

Happy are you if you know how to hold your
    tongue and smile, even when people interrupt
    and contradict you or tread on your toes;
the Gospel has begun to seep into your heart.

Above all, blessed are you who recognise the Lord
    in all whom you meet;
the light of truth shines in your life for you have
    found true wisdom.

Joseph Folliet, d. 1972

6 Belief

I believe in the nothingness of Wrong,
Which holds within itself destruction, death,
Passes ultimately and is no more.

I believe in the liveliness of Joy,
Which thrills with a pulsating urge
Upspringing, vibrating, creative law.

I believe in the tenderness of Love,
Knowing no limits, true, compassionate,
Cherishing, guiding, unlocking every door.

I believe in the sanctity of Truth
Not found, but always searching forendlessly,
Probing deeper into the single core.

I believe in the integrity of Man
Who shrinks with horror at his mirrored self
And hates his future sinking into war.

Katie Jackson

7 Bereavement

Alone yet never quite alone,
I face an empty chair –
But sometimes in the silence,
I imagine you are there.
The good companion of the past,
No longer here with me;
And yet in some mysterious way,
You keep me company.
Thought or spirit?
Does it matter?
Words are meaningless.
I only know that in my times of
    greatest loneliness;
I felt that you are somewhere
    near though nothing's seen or said,
The bitter moment passes and
    my heart is comforted.
I receive the strength I need,
Am rescued from despair;
Maybe that's the way God works
    the answer to a prayer.

Though my loss is grievous and
the future is unknown,
I face the years that lie ahead,
Alone yet not alone.

8 Bereavement

God has not taken them from us.
    He has hidden them in his heart
        That they may be closer to ours.

9 Bereavement

The light goes out of life for us,
The world turns dark and drear,
When God calls unto himself
The ones we hold most dear.
His ways we cannot understand
Because we cannot see
The pattern he is weaving
On the loom of destiny.
But God is good and our grief grows old.
Time plays its gentle part
Laying healing hands upon
The red wounds of the heart.
The secret scars grow fainter
With the passing of the years
And faith returns,
As joy comes back
To wipe away the tears.

10 Bereavement

I miss you every hour of every day,
And yet, dear one, I would not have you stay
If in the years ahead there would be pain
And maybe sorrow to be borne again.

I count my blessings as I call to mind
Our happy hours together, and I find
A bitter sweetness in the lovely hours
That now are all my own, but once were ours.

I do the many tasks which once we shared
And treasure all the things for which you cared,
I conjure up your voice and see your face
And thus can be with you in every place.

My loneliness for you, that like a tide
Engulfs me now and then, I try to hide
Because I know, with joy, one thing is true,
Each passing day is one day nearer you.

I only have to wait, and in my dreams
Relive our happy days, and if it seems
That days go slowly by, I shall not weep
Since I have such a loving tryst to keep.

11 Bereavement

I know well there is no comfort for this pain of parting: the wound always remains, but one learns to bear the pain, and learns to thank God for what he gave, for the beautiful memories of the past, and the yet more beautiful hope for the future.

Max Muller 1862 - 1919

12 | Bible

I have found in it
words for my inmost thoughts,
songs for my joy,
utterance for my hidden griefs, and
pleadings for my shame and feebleness.

Samuel Taylor Coleridge 1772 - 1834

13 | Blessing

May the road rise to meet you.
May the wind be always at your back.
May the sun shine warm upon your face.
May the rains fall softly upon your fields until we
meet again.
May God hold you in the hollow of his hand.

Old Gaelic blessing

14 | Calmness

Be calm, no matter what may befall you. Rest in me.
Be patient, and let patience have her perfect work.
Never think things overwhelming. How can you be
overwhelmed when I am with you?

Do not feel the strain of life. There is not strain for my
children. Do you not see I am a Master Instrument-
maker? Have I not fashioned each part? Do I not know
just what it can bear without a strain? Would I, the
maker of so delicate an instrument, ask anything that
could destroy or strain?

16

No! The strain is only when you are serving another master, the world, fame, the good opinion of men – or carrying two days' burden on the one day.

Remember that it must not be.

from God Calling *a devotional diary by Two Listeners*

15 Caring

When someone cares
it is easier to speak
it is easier to listen
it is easier to play
it is easier to work.

When someone cares
it is easier to laugh.

Susan Polis Schutz

16 Challenge

The ultimate measure of a man is not where he stands in moments of comfort and convenience, but where he stands at times of challenge and controversy.

Martin Luther King 1929 - 1968

17 Changes

It is only when people begin to shake loose from their preoccupations, from the ideas that have dominated them, that we begin to receive a sense of opening, a sense of vision ... That is the sort of time we live in now. We ... live in an epoch in which the solid ground of our preconceived ideas shakes daily under our uncertain feet.

Barbara Ward 1914 -1981

18 Changes

There was a young curate from Dun Laoghaire,
Who stood on his head at the Kyrie,
When the people asked why
He said in reply,
It's the latest liturgical theory!

19 Charity

You are indeed charitable when you give, and while giving, turn your face away so that you may not see the shyness of the receiver.

Kahlil Gibran 1884 - 1931

20 Charter of Belief

I believe that the best way to prepare for a Future Life
    is to be
kind, live one day at a time, and do the work you can
    do best, doing it as well as you can
I believe we should remember the week-day, to keep
    it holy.
I believe that sin is misdirected energy.
I believe that there is no devil but Fear.
I believe that no one can harm you but yourself.
I believe in my own divinity – and yours.

I believe that we are all sons of God, and that it doth
not yet appear what we shall be.

I believe the only way we can reach the Kingdom of
Heaven is to have the Kingdom of Heaven in our
hearts.

I believe in every man minding his own business,
because I believe in freedom – social, economic,
domestic, political, mental, spiritual.

I believe in sunshine, fresh air, friendship, calm sleep,
beautiful thoughts, because it is what we think and
do that makes us what we are.

I believe in the paradox of success through failure;
that death is a manifestation of Life; and that the
universe was planned for good.

Elbert Hubbard 1856 - 1915

21 | Children

And a woman who held a babe against her
bosom said:
Speak to us of Children.
And he said:
Your children are not your children.
They are the sons and daughters of Life's longing for
itself.
They come through you but not from you
And though they are with you yet they belong not to
you.
You may give them your love but not your thoughts.
For they have their own thoughts.
You may house their bodies but not their soul,
For their souls dwell in the house of tomorrow,
which you cannot visit, not even in your dreams.
You may strive to be like them, but seek not to
make them like you.
For life goes not backward nor tarries with yester-
day.

You are the bows from which your children as living
    arrows are sent forth.
The archer sees the mark upon the path of the
    infinite, and he bends you with his might that his
    arrows may go swift and far.
Let your bending in the Archer's hand be for glad-
    ness;
For even as he loves the arrow that flies, so he loves
    also the bow that is stable.

Kahlil Gibran 1884 - 1931

22 Children

The Beauty of a Child

In the face of a child,
see the beauty of God,
of the clear graceful wonder,
of life and creation.

In the eyes of the child
see the seeking of love,
the want of affection
of those whom they love.

There is no fear of exposure
in their sharing of joy,
for they have not encountered
life's pain or its wounds.

Their adventure is endless
as they seek our response
to the arms ever open
for a gentle embrace.

The years will soon form them,
the first steps grow firm,

friendships will bond them,
and life's journey begin.

If life did not hurt us
or pain mar our joy,
we would not encounter
our goal or reward.

It is the events of our living,
the trials and our joys,
that gives life its meaning,
so that man can survive.

Brother Cornelius Kearney

23 | Children

From the creatures of God man can learn wisdom;
and he can apply to himself the instruction they give.
Go into the desert, my son. Watch the young stork of
the wilderness, and let him speak to your heart. He
bears his aged parent between his wings; he carries
him into safety – and he supplies him with food. Be
grateful, then, to your father, for he gave you life; and
likewise to your mother, for she nurtured you and
sustained you.

When your parents utter words of reproof, they are
spoken for your own good, so listen to their admoni-
tion, for it does not proceed from malice, but is pro-
vided by love,

Your parents have watched over your welfare, and
they have toiled that life shall be easier for you. Hon-
our them, therefore, in their age; and let them not be
treated with irreverence.

21

They ask no reward for what they have done for you;
but see that you do not repay them with ingratitude.
Think back on the years of your helpless infancy, lest
you forget to help them through the infirmities of the
decline of life.

So shall their heads go down to the grave in peace;
and your own children, in reverence of your own
example, will do the same for you.

Dandemis, 3rd century B.C.

24 Choice

We cannot chose the best.
    The Best chooses us.

Rabindranath Tagore 1861 - 1941

25 Christian

Christian: One who believes that the New Testament
is a divinely inspired book admirably suited to the
spiritual needs of his neighbour.

Ambrose Bierce 1842 - 1914

26 Christianity

The spiritual life
is, first of all, life.
To be a Christian
is to experience life at its different levels,
to understand that experience
in the light of the gospel,
and to bring to bear the energies and resources

of Christian spirituality
so that in each experience
we rise above the destructive forces
that isolate and alienate from environment, self,
others and God
and move
from isolation to community
from selfishness to service and
from fragmentary existence to faithful loving.

Donal Spring

27 Christianity

Most people really believe that the Christian commandments (e.g., to love one's neighbour as oneself) are
intentionally a little too severe – like putting the clock
ahead half an hour to make sure of not being late in
the morning.

Sören Kierkegaard 1813 - 1855

23 Christianity

One of the surprising and unique faculties of the
Christian religion is its ability to guide and console
anyone who has recourse to it in any juncture or di-
lemma whatsoever. If there is any remedy for the past,
it prescribes and supplies it, gives the light and strength
to apply it, whatever the cost: if there is none, it provides the means of carrying out in reality the proverb
about making a virtue of necessity. It teaches people
to pursue steadily what they have begun lightly: it
inclines the mind to accept willingly what has been
imposed by force, and gives to a rash but irrevocable
choice all the sanctity, all the wisdom, and let us even
say boldly, all the joys of a vocation. It is a path so

made that by whatever labyrinth or precipice man may reach it, once he takes the first step, he can thenceforward walk safely and cheerfully along it and arrive happily at a happy end.

Alessandro Manzoni

29 Comfort

Blessed be the God and Father of our Lord Jesus Christ, the Father of mercies and God of all comfort, who comforts us in all our affliction, so that we may be able to comfort those who are in any affliction, with the comfort with which we ourselves are comforted by God. For as we share abundantly in Christ's sufferings, so through Christ we share abundantly in comfort too.

2 Corinthians 1:3-5

30 Comfort

We often find comfort in telling
    what is painful in actual experience.

St Basil c. 330-379

31 Commandments

My Ten Commandments

Thou shalt not worry, for worry is the most unproductive of all human activities.

Thou shalt not be fearful, for most of the things we fear never come to pass.

Thou shalt not cross bridges before you get to them, for no one yet has succeeded in accomplishing this.

Thou shalt face each problem as it comes. You can handle only one at a time anyway.

Thou shalt not take problems to bed with you for they make very poor bedfellows.

Thou shalt not borrow other people's problems. They can take better care of them than you can.

Thou shalt not try to relive yesterday for good or ill – it is gone. Concentrate on what is happening in your life today.

Thou shalt count thy blessings, never overlooking the small ones, for a lot of small blessings add up to a big one.

Thou shalt be a good listener, for only when you listen do you hear ideas different from your own. It's very hard to learn something new when you're talking.

Thou shalt not become bogged down by frustration, for 90 percent of it is rooted in self-pity and it will only interfere with positive action.

Elodie Armstrong

February

1 | Commendation

A prayer for loved ones

We thank you, Our Father, that our loved ones
who have gone from our sight are in your keeping.
Help us to leave them there in perfect trust,
because you love them and us with infinite love.
Grant that we may learn to know you better,
so that we may meet them again in your presence,
through faith in him who loved us and gave himself
for us, Jesus Christ our Saviour.

R.E. Cleeve

2 | Commendation as death approaches

Lord, you have loved me and have supported me all the
days of my life, and I trust you. Now that the time of my
death approaches, give me faith to trust you still and to
know that you will continue to support me as you have
always done. Death like life comes from you and like
all your gifts must be good, so take away any fears I
may have. When death comes to hush my last breath
on earth, help me to remember that it will bring me to
live more fully with you and this is the most wonderful
thing that can happen to me; so into your hands I
commend my spirit.

Michael Hollings and Etta Gullick

3 | Commendation

Go forth, Christian soul, from this world
in the name of God the almighty Father,
who created you,

in the name of Jesus Christ, Son of the living God,
who suffered for you,
in the name of the Holy Spirit,
who was poured out upon you.
Go forth, faithful Christian.

May you live in peace this day,
may your home be with God in Zion,
with Mary, the virgin Mother of God,
with Joseph, and all the angels and saints.

*This beautiful prayer is said by a priest for the
commendation of a dying person*

4 | Communion

Always seek communion. It is the most precious thing
men possess. In this respect, the symbol of the religions
is indeed full of- majesty. Where there is communion
there is something that is more than human, there is
surely something divine.

Georges Duhamel 1884 - 1966

5 | Compassion

Compassion is a word full of meaning.
It means:
sharing the same passion,
sharing the same suffering,
sharing the same agony,
accepting into my heart
the misery in yours.

Your pain calls out to me.
It touches my heart.

It awakens something within me,
and I become one with you in your pain.

I may not be able to relieve your pain,
but by understanding it and sharing it
I make it possible for you to bear it
in a way that enhances your dignity
and helps you to grow.

Jean Vanier

6 Compassion

I feel your pain
and long to touch the hurt
and make it melt away.
Yes, I know
that I can't really see
the breadth
and depth
of this dark valley you're in.
I can't truly know
just how sharp the knife is
in your soul –
for it is you in its path,
not me.
But I have known other valleys,
and in my heart
still bear knife-wound scars.
Even so,
I would walk your road
and take your pain
if I could.
I cannot.
And yet, perhaps
in some way
I can be a hand to hold
in the darkness:

in some way, try to blunt
the sharpness of pain.
But if not –
it may help a little
just to know I care.

Christine Rigden

7 | Confidence

The confidence which we have in ourselves gives birth
to much of that which we have in others.

François de la Rochefoucauld 1613 - 1680

8 | Cross, The

The Christian who desires to follow Jesus carrying his
cross must bear in mind that the name "Christian" means
"learner or imitator of Christ" and that if he wishes to
bear that noble title worthily he must above all do as
Christ charges us in the Gospel: we must oppose or
deny ourselves, take up the cross, and follow him.

St Anthony Mary Claret 1807 - 1870

9 | Cross

If we had it in our power to create new worlds of
beauty, hills and valleys of a thousand royal hues:

If we gained the greatest riches from all corners of the
earth, ours to give away as we might choose:

If we wrote the most majestic and the sweetest sounds
of music that would echo throughout all eternity,

29

Or could pen the words of genius that would turn the world around and go on to change the course of history:

If we offered up our homes, our lands, and even those we love, as small payment, never thinking of our loss,

We could count it all as worthless, for there's nothing we can give to thank the Lord our loving Saviour, for the cross.

10 Cross

Splinters from the Cross

Little headaches, little heartaches,
Little griefs of every day.
Little trials and vexations
How they throng around our way.
One great cross, immense and heavy
So it seems to our weak will,
Might be borne with resignation
But these small ones kill.
Yet all life is formed of small things.
Little leaves make up the trees,
Many tiny drops of water
Blending, make the mighty seas.
Let us not then by impatience
Mar the beauty of the whole,
But for the love of Jesus bear all
In the silence of the soul.
Asking him for grace sufficient
To sustain us through each loss,
And to treasure each small offering
As a splinter from his Cross.

11 | Crucifix, The

The crucifix – I dreaded what I felt it demanded of me. And since I have been a Carmelite, the crucifix I received at my profession has never left me. It is always the faithful friend, the confidant of every hour, joyful or sad. But it is "of the night" – in naked faith. Yet every day we are becoming more intimate, my crucifix and I, even when no word is spoken. Silence can sometimes be more eloquent than words. And at prayer, when aridity or dryness, or the fear of losing or abandoning God grips us until we are in an agony, the only refuge is to take our crucifix and look at it, to cling to it with a simple look, as a shipwrecked person clings to a plank, and try to place in it all our confidence, faith and love. How often I have found salvation in the crucifix in this way, and at the same time peace, and the strength to start again.

72 year-old Carmelite (43 years in religion)

12 | Deaf, The

Blessed are they who seem to know...
    That lip-reading is difficult and slow.

Blessed are they who shake my hand...
    and write notes to help me understand.

Blessed are they who know that I long
    To hear voices, music and song.

Blessed are they who seem to see...
    When I'm lost in a group of two or three.

Blessed are they who take time out...
    To explain to me what they are talking about.

Blessed are they who are patient and kind...
    That give me comfort and peace of mind.

Blessed are they who have a smile...
That makes my life more worthwhile.

Blessed are they who make it known
By faith in God's promises: I'll not walk alone...

Blessed are they who understand...
As I journey to that City "not made with hands".

13 Death

In a good old age, Death, the friend, came and opened the door of this mortal state, and a great soul that served a long apprenticeship to little things, went forth into the joy of its Lord; a life of self-sacrifice and self-abnegation passed into a life of endless rest.

Harriet Beecher Stowe 1811 - 1896

14 Death

If I should never see the moon again
Rising red gold across the harvest field,
Or feel the stinging of soft April rain
As the brown earth her hidden treasures yield:

If I should never hear the thrushes wake
Long before the sunrise in the glittering dawn,
Or watch the huge Atlantic rollers break
Against the rugged cliffs in baffling scorn:

If I have said goodbye to stream and wood,
To the wide ocean and the green clad hill,
I know that he who made this world so good
Has somewhere made a heaven better still.

This I bear witness with my latest breath:
Knowing the love of God I fear not death.

Major Malcolm Boyd (killed on D-Day)

15 Death

At the heart of the Christian faith is the conviction that, when death is accepted in a spirit of faith, and when one's whole life is oriented to self-giving so that at its end one gladly and freely surrenders it back into the hands of God the Creator and Redeemer, then death is transformed into a fulfillment. One conquers death by love – not by one's own heroic virtuousness, but by sharing in that love with which Christ accepted death on the Cross. This is not apparent to reason: it is, precisely, a matter of faith.

Thomas Merton 1915 - 1968

16 Death

Stephen Cummins, aged 24, a British soldier who was killed in Northern Ireland, left this poem in an envelope for his parents, which should only be opened in the event of his death. It was his farewell message of comfort and hope to them.

Do not stand at my grave and weep
I am not there. I do not sleep.
I am a thousand winds that blow.
I am the diamond glints on snow.
I am the sunlight on ripened grain.
I am the gentle autumn rain.
When you awaken in the morning's hush,
I am the swift uplifting rush
of quiet birds in circled flight.

I am the soft stars that shine at night.
Do not stand at my grave and cry.
I am not there; I did not die.

Anon.

17 Death

An Indian prayer

When I am dead, cry for me a little,
Think of me sometimes, but not too much,
Think of me now and again, as I was in life.
At some moment it's pleasant to recall,
But not for long.
Leave me in peace, and I shall leave you in peace.
And while you live, let your thoughts be with the
living.

Anon.

18 Death

Death is only a level-crossing from one life to
    another;
from life in its beginnings to life in full achievement;
from this incomplete life to that transformed one.
For the true Christian, death has the character of any
    other
natural event – no longer agonising or tragic,
    because decisive.

Raoul Plus SJ

34

19 | Death

I believe in death.
I believe it is part of life.
I believe that we are born to die;
—to die that we may live more fully:
born to die a little each day —
to selfishness, to pretence and to sin.
I believe that every time we pass
from one stage of life to another,
something in us dies and something new is born.
I believe we taste death in moments
of loneliness and rejection,
in moments of sorrow and disappointment,
when we are afraid, lose courage, and give up;
when we see our dreams broken,
and every time we say "Goodbye"
I believe, too, that we are dying before our time
when we live in bitterness, in hatred and isolation.
I believe that each day we are creating our own
    death —
by the way we live.
To those who believe in Christ, death is a gateway
    to eternal life.

20 | Death

Death is the gateway to eternal life

Death is just another step along life's changing way,
no more than just a gateway to a new and better
    day,
and parting from our loved ones is much easier to
    bear
when we know that they are waiting for us to join
    them "There"

for it is on the Wings of Death that the living soul
takes flight
into the "Promised Land of God" where there shall
be "No Night"
so death is just a natural thing, like the closing of a
door,
as we start upon a journey to a new and distant
shore
and none need make this journey undirected or
alone,
for God promised us safe passage to this vast and
great unknown
so let your grief be softened and yield not to
despair,
you have only placed your loved one in the loving
Father's care.

Helen Steiner Rice

21 Death

It's not that I'm afraid to die.
I just don't want to be there when it happens!

Woody Allen

22 Death

The doctrine of the inevitability of death for all living
creatures is movingly expressed in one of the most
popular of all Buddhist stories, the "Parable of the
Mustard Seed." According to this story, a woman is
discovered grieving uncontrollably over the death of
her beloved son whose corpse she carries in her arms.
She does not seem to be aware that death is a terminal
event, for this lifetime at least. In hopes of finding an

antidote to her child's malady which would restore him
to consciousness, she approached the Buddha who is
renowned for his miraculous powers to heal. The Buddha
does provide her with an antidote, but not the kind she
has sought. He instructs her to go from house to house
throughout the city in search of a few grains of mustard
seed. The mustard seed, he says, will provide the proper
antidote to the child's disease (i.e., death). But she must
accept the mustard seed only from a household in
which no-one has ever died – not a father or a mother,
not a brother or sister, not a servant or animal. After
searching from house to house, she discovers that not
a single household can be found which has never
experienced the death of one of its members. In time
she comes to see the truth which is the panacea to
death and sorrow; that death is the inescapable destiny
of all creatures and that, given its inevitability, she has
no cause to grieve. Relieved from the pangs of both
false hope and needless grief, she goes immediately
with peace of mind to the burning ground and there
submits her son to the fires of cremation.

23 Death

Often fill your mind with thoughts of the great gentleness and mercy with which God our Saviour welcomes
souls at death, if they have spent their lives in trusting
him, and striven to serve and love him. Do your utmost
to arouse in yourself a love of heaven and the life of the
blessed so you will weaken your dread of parting from
this mortal and fleeting life.

St Francis de Sales 1567 - 1622

24 Death

There may be a wonderful completeness in a life which lasted only a few years.

Dean W.R. Inge 1860 - 1954

25 Death

If I should die before the rest of you
Break not a flower nor inscribe a stone
Nor, when I'm gone, speak in a Sunday voice,
But be the usual selves that I have known.

Weep if you must.
Parting is hell.
But life goes on.
So sing as well.

Joyce Grenfell 1910 - 1979

26 Death

Welcome into your kingdom our departed brothers
and sisters,
and all who have left this world in your friendship.
There we hope to share in your glory
when every tear will be wiped away.
On that day we shall see you, our God, as you are.
We shall become like you and praise you
forever through Christ our Lord,
from whom all good things come.

from Eucharistic Prayer III

27 | Development

Let us always remember that in human affairs there is no possibility of success without continual development, and that not to walk is to fall.

Frédéric Ozanam 1813 - 1853

28 | Dialogue

Man is made for dialogue ... and the man who does not talk to others, who is not open to reality, does not listen, does not answer, is like a plant denied nourishment from the soil.

Cardinal Agostino Casaroli

29 | (leap year)

Disillusionment

The law of disillusionment with the world is the introduction to all spiritual life, and is a fact to be joyfully accepted, meditated upon, and made a matter of thanksgiving to almighty God.

Man made in God's image can only rest in God, and is irrevocably doomed to be disappointed with anything else.

The deeper the disillusionment is, the deeper will be the service it may render to the spiritual life.

Let us begin then by welcoming disillusionment. Let us follow it steadily as it leads through disgust and disappointment with one thing after another – disgust and disappointment with the transitory, the disconnected, and the imperfect, to the threshold of the spiritual life. This discontent is a divine discontent; its function is to bring us to the one, unchanging, and eternal Christ.

Bishop Arthur Chandler 1860 - 1939

March

1 Easter

Judas betrayed him and Peter denied him;
Other disciples forsook him and fled.
Would I have been braver, if I had been present,
And stayed with my Lord who so soon would be
dead?

Caiaphas plotted, and Herod derided;
Pilate condemned him to hang on the tree.
In their position I might have done likewise,
Never imagining this was for me.

Mary mistook him, and Thomas was doubting,
Paul dragged his followers bound into jail.
How do I meet the New Testament challenge?
Could I succeed where such characters fail?

Jesus forgave them – the thief on the gallows,
The soldiers who killed him, and Peter his friend.
His love did not fail in a world black with hatred.
His love drew men back to his side in the end.

Two thousand Easters have gone like a shadow.
This is our moment in history's screed.
Jesus our Lover is calling us forward;
Through him, and only through him, we succeed.

June Chantry

2 Easter

We all experience moments of dying in our lives.
We get a foretaste of death
when we live in bitterness,

when prejudice blinds us,
when loneliness enfolds us,
when fears oppress us,
when sadness overwhelms us,
and when we give in to despair.
In those moments the world is closing in on us,
and we have one foot in the grave already.

But we also experience moments of resurrection in
    our lives:
when we know true love,
when we are accepted,
when we are forgiven,
when we open our hearts to our neighbour,
and when hope returns.
In those moments our horizon is widening
and we are emerging from the tomb.

Lord Jesus,
may the power of your resurrection touch whatever
    is dead in us
and bring it back to life.
Let the splendour of your resurrection light up the
    world,
scattering the shadows of death
and helping all of the Father's children
to walk in radiant hope towards the kingdom that is
    to come.

Flor McCarthy SDB

3 | Education

If you give a man a fish, he will eat once,
If you teach a man to fish, he will eat for the rest of
    his life.
If you are thinking a year ahead, sow seed,

If you are thinking ten years ahead, plant a tree.
If you are thinking one hundred years ahead, edu-
cate the people.
By sowing the seed, you will harvest once.
By planting a tree, you will harvest tenfold.
By educating the people, you will harvest one hun-
dredfold.

Kuang-tsu, 3rd century B.C.

4 Enthusiasm

The Greeks understood the mysterious power of the
hidden side of things. They bequeathed to us one of the
most beautiful words in our language – the word
"enthusiasm" – en theos – the god within.

Louis Pasteur 1886 - 1970

5 Envy

It is enough if you don't freeze in the cold, and if thirst
and hunger don't claw at your insides. If your back isn't
broken, if your feet can walk, if both arms can bend,
if both eyes can see and if both ears can hear, then
whom should you envy? And why? Our envy of others
devours us most of all. Rub your eyes and purify your
heart and prize above all else in the world those who
love you and wish you well. After all, it may be your last
act.

Alexander Solzhenitsyn

6 Epitaph

Here lies a poor woman, who always was tired;
She lived in a house where help was not hired.

Her last words on earth were: "Dear friends, I am
    going
Where washing ain't done, nor sweeping, nor
    sewing:
But everything is exactly to my wishes;
For where they don't eat there's no washing of
    dishes,
I'll be where loud anthems will always be ringing,
But having no voice, I'll be clear of the singing.
Don't mourn for me now; don't mourn for me
    never –
I'm going to do nothing for ever and ever."

The Tired Woman's Epitaph
said to date from 1744, from Bushey, Hertfordshire

7 Eucharist

Be gentle
When you touch bread.
Let it not lie
Uncared for – unwanted.
So often bread
Is taken for granted.
There is much beauty in bread.
Beauty of sun and soil,
Beauty of patient toil,
Winds and rain have caressed it.
Christ often blessed it.
Be gentle
When you touch bread.

8 Failure

And then he allows some of us to fall more severely and
distressingly than before – at least that is how we see
it. And then it seems to us, who are not always wise,
that all we set our hands to is lost. But it is not so. We

44

need to fall, and we need to see that we have done so. For if we never fell we should not know how weak and pitiable we are in ourselves. Nor should we fully know the wonderful love of our Maker.

In heaven we shall see truly and everlastingly that we have grievously sinned in this life; notwithstanding, we shall see that this in no way diminished his love, nor made us less precious in his sight.

The testing experience of falling will lead us to a deep and wonderful knowledge of the constancy of God's love, which neither can nor will be broken because of sin. To understand this is of great profit.

Julian of Norwich c. 1342 - after 1413

9 | Faith

That man is perfect in faith who can come to God in the utter dearth of his feelings and desires, without a glow or an aspiration, with the weight of low thoughts, failures, neglects, and wandering forgetfulness, and say to him, "Thou art my refuge".

George MacDonald 1824 - 1905

10 | Faith

If it were given to us to know
the whole of life's unfolding plan –
If we could see what waits for us
out there beyond our little span –
there'd be no lovely mystery,
no wonder at the heart of things –
for we with open eyes would see
the answer to our questionings.
It's well God keeps his secrets, for
if everything we knew –
where would be the need of faith
to strive for ends beyond our view?

45

It is enough to know that he
is there, below and above;
that all the boundless universe
is in his hands ...
      and he is love.

11 Fear

The wise man in the storm prays God, not for safety
from danger, but for deliverance from fear. It is the
storm within which endangers him, not the storm
without.

Ralph Waldo Emerson 1803 - 1882

12 Fear

Lord, it would be idle
to pretend that I have no fears;
Even tho' I am full of faith
And I am mindful of thy mercy,
And I am hedged about
By your almighty assurances,
I still advance towards you
With joy and anticipation
And fear of the uncharted seas.
Although I know not the day
Of your beckoning, my faith tells me
To mark off the days like a homesick
Schoolboy puts pen through the days
Separating him from homecoming.
So I, above all, long for the freedom
Of the sons of God. Lord, give me
Inward peace, take away all fear.

Sidney G. Reeman
a poem written shortly before his death in 1975

13 Forgiveness

When, through my tears, I began to tell him (Jesus) something of the years during which I betrayed him, he lovingly placed his hand over my mouth in order to silence me. His concern was that I should muster enough courage to pick myself up again to try to carry on walking, in spite of my weakness, and to believe in his love in spite of my fears.

Carlo Carretto

14 Forgiveness

A hymn to God the Father

Wilt Thou forgive that sin where I begun,
Which was my sin, though it were done before?
Wilt Thou forgive that sin, through which I run,
And do run still, though still I do deplore?
When Thou hast done, Thou hast not done,
For I have more.
Wilt Thou forgive that sin by which I have won
Others to sin, and made my sin their door?
Wilt Thou forgive that sin which I did shun
A year, or two: but wallowed in, a score?
When Thou hast done, Thou hast not done,
For I have more.
I have a sin of fear, that when I have spun
My last thread, I shall perish on the shore;
But swear by Thy self, that at my death Thy Son
Shall shine as he shines now, and heretofore;
And, having done that, Thou hast done;
I fear no more.

John Donne 1573 - 1631

15 Forgiveness

The quicker we are to discover our secret faults, the more do we need, if we are to avoid becoming obsessed by them, to understand the immensity of God's forgiveness. He asks us to recognise them, and humbly to turn away from them, solely in order for us to understand our poverty and his mercy, not so that we shall carry on in the utopian hope that we can ever act without sin entering into our action. "When we are in doubt as to whether we have offended God," says St Francis de Sales, "we must humble ourselves, request God to excuse us, and ask for more enlightenment for another time, and forget completely what has happened and return to our accustomed way. For an inquisitive and anxious search to know whether we have acted rightly, indubitably arises from self-love."

Paul Tournier 1905 - 1986

16 Forgiveness

When God pardons, he consigns the offence to everlasting forgetfulness.

Mary Rosell

17 Forgiveness

O God,

We remember not only our son but also his murderers;

Not because they killed him in the prime of his youth and made our hearts bleed and our tears flow,

Not because with this savage act they have brought further disgrace on the name of our country among the civilized nations of the world;

But because through their crime we now follow thy footsteps more closely in the way of sacrifice.

The terrible fire of this calamity burns up all selfishness and possessiveness in us;

Its flame reveals the depth of depravity and meanness and suspicion, the dimension of hatred and the measure of sinfulness in human nature;

It makes obvious as never before our need to trust in God's love as shown in the cross of Jesus and his resurrection;

Love which makes us free from hate towards our persecutors;

Love which brings patience, forbearance, courage, loyalty, humility, generosity, greatness of heart;

Love which more than ever deepens our trust in God's final victory and his eternal designs for the Church and for the world;

Love which teaches us how to prepare ourselves to face our own day of death.

O God,

Our son's blood has multiplied the fruit of the Spirit in the soil of our souls;

So when his murderers stand before thee on the day of judgement

Remember the fruit of the Spirit by which they have enriched our lives.

And forgive.

Bishop Dehqani-Tafti of Iran

18 | Forgiveness

Reconciliation is no mere ceremony.
It is a necessary part of every Christian Life, and
   where the Holy Spirit moves a person in this undertaking,

then it must be seen through to its completion,
    however painful the undertaking proves to be.
God is fully aware of all those dark corners,
hidden from the sights of others,
and before a person is able to fully undertake
the work that has been assigned to him or her,
these corners must be cleansed – and forgiven.

Patricia Vardigans

19 Friendship

A friend is one who knows you as you are,
Understands where you've been,
Accepts who you've become.
And still invites you to grow.

20 Friendship

People need people
and friends need friends
and we all need love
for a full life depends
just in knowing
that someone cares
and holds us close
in their thoughts and prayers.

21 Friendship

Do not make friends with any persons except those
whom you can help or those who can help you and
animate you, by word and example, to love Jesus and
live in his spirit.

St John Eudes 1601 - 1680

22 | Friendship

The highest privilege there is, is the privilege of being allowed to share another's pain. You talk about your pleasures to your acquaintances: you talk about your troubles to your friends.

Fr Andrew SDC

23 | Friendship

The disciples at Emmaus, we are told, know him in the breaking of bread. It is the symbol of hospitality, of friendship. And we, if we are to live consciously in his companionship, must give him the marks of our friendship in our turn. Now I call you not servants but friends, he explicitly told his disciples; we have only to do our part ... not just a sharing of superficialities such as exists between acquaintances, but a sharing of the deep things of life, the deep thoughts and ambitions, the secrets of the heart. Our Lord, for his part, calls us not servants but friends, because, he says, he has made known to us the secrets of his own heart, has shown us the plot of his own love-story: it only remains for us to do the same.

Gerald Vann OP 1906 - 1963

24 | Friendship

What a mystery friendship is! One of those subtle and beautiful forces that glorify life. And how strangely and delightfully different one's friends are one from the other – not only in themselves, but in the way one has to look at them. Some we have to carry, while others carry us. The perfect friend, to my mind, is one who believes in one once and for all, and never requires explanations and assurances.

Dame Laurentia McLachlan OSB 1866 - 1953

25 | Friendship

No medicine is more valuable, none more efficacious, none better suited to the cure of all our temporal ills than a friend, to whom we may turn for consolation in time of trouble, and with whom we may share our happiness in time of joy.

St Aelred of Rievaulx 1109 - 1167

26 | Friendship

True friends visit us in prosperity only when invited,
but in adversity they come without invitation.

Theophrastus 350 B.C. - 285 B.C.

27 | Friendship

I want to love you without clutching,
Appreciate you without judging,
Join you without invading,
Invite you without demanding,
Leave you without guilt,
Criticise you without blaming,
and help you without insulting.
If I can have the same from YOU
then we can truly meet and enrich each other.

Virginia Satir

28 | Friendship

Of all things which wisdom provides to make life entirely happy,
    much the greatest is the possession of friendship.

Epicurus 341 B.C. - 270 B.C.

29 | Friendship

If a man does not make new acquaintances as he advances through life, he will soon find himself left alone. A man, sir, should keep his friendships in constant repair.

Samuel Johnson 1709 - 1784

30 | Friendship

I thank you for my friends, for those who understand me better than I understand myself, for those who know me at my worst and still like me, for those who have forgiven me when I had no right to expect to be forgiven. Help me to be as true to my friends as I would wish them to be to me.

William Barclay 1907 - 1978

31 | Friendship

With every true friendship we build more firmly the foundations on which the peace of the whole world rests.

Mahatma Gandhi 1869 - 1948

1   Generosity

Bernard introduced himself and told me that he was registered blind. He mentioned that he had another blind friend who had been extremely good to him, and when she died the minister at her funeral service ended his homily with the words "And she was one of those people in life – who did walk the extra mile." Those words stuck in Bernard's mind and inspired him to write this poem. On a recent visit to Lourdes he had copies made for his fellow pilgrims, and the spiritual leader of the group was so impressed that he asked Bernard to recite it from memory, during Mass at the Poor Clare Convent.

The extra mile

Dear Lord, I find it hard to give
As you have told me to.
To make the smallest sacrifice
Sometimes is hard to do.
So grant me, Lord, the gift to give,
And through my self denial,
Lord Jesus, in my love for you,
I'll walk the Extra Mile.

Lord, give my eyes the gift to see
The other person's need
And take from me my selfishness,
Self-centredness and greed,
And make my ears attentive
To the hard cry of despair.
Lord, grant that I will go without
While others have my share.

My hands, dear Lord, are idle
And I offer them to you
That you may use them as you will.
There's so much they can do.
And guide my feet that I will walk
With those who walk alone.

And may my footprints on this earth
Lead to your Heavenly Throne.

Oh Lord, if I can live this way
My life will be worthwhile,
For then I'd know that in your name
I walk the Extra Mile
For I remember long ago that day on Calvary
Those many many extra miles, dear Lord,
You walked for me. Amen.

Bernard Boon

2 Gentleness

Meekness was the method that Jesus used with the apostles. He put up with their ignorance and roughness and even their infidelity. He treated sinners with a kindness and affection that caused some to be shocked, others to be scandalized, and still others to gain hope in God's mercy. Thus, he bade us to be gentle and humble of heart.

St John Bosco 1815 - 1888

3 Giving

If you give something to someone who is in need then let a cheerful face precede your gift, along with kind words and encouragement for his suffering.

When you do this, the pleasure he feels in his mind at your gift will be greater than the needs of his body.

A person who, while having God in mind, honours everyone, will find everyone to be his helper, thanks to the hidden will of God.

Someone who speaks in defence of a person who suffers injustice will find an advocate in his Creator.

Whoever gives a hand to help his neighbour is helped by God's own hand.

But the person who accuses his brother for his evil deeds will find God as his accuser.

Isaac of Syria, 7th century

4 Giving

The truth is that human beings are only at peace with themselves, and therefore contented, when they feel that they are giving more than they are taking, not because they are compelled to give, but because they want to.

Sir Arthur Bryant

5 God

God can build from a broken life,
Can resurrect those first great hopes
And bring them to fulfilment.
What man has marred,
That God can work on,
Till the finished work
Of Creator's hand
Is as the Creator
Intended it to be.

Despair not, men of clay;
Fear not, O you who see your loss
With terror and a hopeless heart.
We cannot do what God can do;
We cannot build upon a base of sin.

But God can take that base
And in his grace
Can fill the life within
With working, leavening, pulsating
Action.
So rotted root doth nonetheless
Become God's beauty tree,
And sin forgiven is transformed
Entire.

Robina Knewstub

6 | God

If God is with us,
it will be accomplished.

Blessed Jeanne Jugan 1792 - 1879

7 | God

"I am your God"

I am your God ... and I stand close by you ... Is not this enough? ... What more do you desire on earth than my love, of which my heart is full?

I am your God ... and I remain faithful to you, even when I send you sorrows; remember only that I am with you ... What more do you desire? ...

I am your God ... and I think of you ... From all eternity I have thought of you; I have written your name in the depths of my heart in order that I might never forget you ...

I am your God ... and I arrange all for your happiness; if you do not understand now, one day you shall see clearly ...

I am your God ... and I truly love you ... I know all that grieves you ... I see every glance, I hear every word that pains you ...

Accept all with tranquillity and peace, because I myself have allowed and ordered all; you, be faithful to me and persevere, and I shall reward you for all ...

I am your God ... Are you alone? ... I shall be your friend. No one speaks kindly to you? ... Come close to me and I shall be your All in the Blessed Sacrament ... I shall be to you a compensation for all that the world denies you ...

I am your God ... What more do you desire? ... Be of good cheer ... May nothing seem too hard for you, because he who possesses my heart and my love has all that he needs ...

The world passes away ... Time is fleeting ... Men forsake one ... Death shall carry off everything from you ... One Thing alone shall always remain to you ... YOUR GOD ...

8 | God

I have no other helper than you, no other Father, I
    pray to you.
Only you can help me. My present misery is too
    great.
Despair grips me, and I am at my wit's end.
O Lord, Creator, Ruler of the world, Father,
I thank you that you have brought me through.
How strong the pain was – but you were stronger.
How deep the fall was – but you were even deeper.
How dark the night was – but you were the noon-
    day sun in it.
You are our father, our mother, our brother, and our
    friend.

African prayer

9 God

> Seek more for the God of consolation
> than the consolations of God.
>
> *Chautard*

10 God

God is Love and he enfoldeth
all the world in one embrace.
With unfailing grasp he holdeth
every child of every race.
And when human hearts are breaking
under sorrow's iron rod
Then they will find the self same aching
deep within the heart of God.

11 God

Pickets at the church gate

How good it is that God alone has never gone on
  strike.
If only he had given up and said "That's it", I'm
  through,
I've had enough of those on earth, so this is what I'll
  do:

"I'll give my orders to the sun – cut off the heat
  supply,
To the moon – give no more light and run the
  oceans dry.
Then just to make things really tough and put the
  pressure on,
Turn off the vital oxygen till every breath is gone."

You know he would be justified if fairness was the
   game
Because he was not treated fair in things he didn't
   like.
No one has been more abused or met with more
   disdain
Than God, and yet he carries on, supplying you and
   me
With all the favours of his grace and everything free.

Men say they want a better deal. But what a deal
   we've
Given God, to whom all things we owe,
We don't care who we hurt to gain the things we
   like,
But what a mess we'd all be in
If God should go on strike.

12 | God

This, then, is what I pray kneeling before the Father,
from whom every family, whether spiritual or natural,
takes its name:

Out of his infinite glory may he give you the power
through his Spirit for your hidden self to grow strong,
so that Christ may live in your hearts through faith, and
then, planted in love and built on love, you will with
all the saints have the strength to grasp the breadth and
the length, the height and the depth; until knowing the
love of Christ which is beyond all knowledge you are
filled with the utter fullness of God.

Glory be to him whose power working in us can do
infinitely more than we can ask or imagine.

Glory be to him from generation to generation in the Church and in Christ Jesus for ever and ever. Amen.

Ephesians 3:14-21
(included as a tribute to Eileen Veronica Law, RIP)

13 God

May he support us all the day long, till the shadows lengthen and the evening comes, and the busy world is hushed, and the fever of life is over, and our work is done! Then in his mercy, may he give us safe lodging, and a holy rest and peace at the last.

Cardinal John Henry Newman 1801 - 1890

14 God

No, I shall never believe in:
the God incapable of giving an answer to the grave problems of a sincere and honest man who cries out in tears: "I can't!"
the God who loves pain,
the God who makes himself feared, ...

the God who has no forgiveness for some sins,
the God who "causes" cancer or "makes" a woman sterile,
the God who does not save those who have not known him but who have desired and searched for him,
the God who does not go out to meet him who had abandoned him,
the God incapable of making everything new,
the God who does not have a different, personal, individual word for each person,
the God who has never wept for men,

the God who cannot find himself in the eyes of a child
    or a pretty woman or a mother in tears,
the God who destroys the earth and the things that man
    loves instead of transforming them,
the God who will accept as a friend anyone who goes
    through the world without making anybody happy,
the God incapable of making man divine and seating
    him at his table and giving him part of his heritage,
the God who is not love and who does not know how
    to transform into love everything he touches,
the God incapable of captivating man's heart,
the God who would not have become a man, with all
    that that implies,
the God who would not have given men even his very
    own mother,
the God in whom I cannot hope against all hope.
Yes, my God is the other God.

Juan Arias

15 God

The only God worth believing in is the God who believed enough in people to die for us. The only God
worth living for is the One who calls us to live with him,
through dark faith in this life, and beyond death in face-
to-face fullness. The only God worth searching for is
the one who searched for us and who still struggles
within us in order that we may become more free to
love.

*Pastoral Letter by the Irish Bishops' Conference
to mark the International Year of Youth in 1985*

16 God

Within the dark chaos of a troubled world
    I will seek and find some Beauteous Thing.

From eyes grown dim with weeping will shine a
    Light to guide me, and in Sorrow's Hour
    I shall behold a great High Courage.

I shall find the wonder of an Infinite Patience,
    and a quiet Faith in coming Joy and Peace.

And Love will I seek in the midst of Discord, and
    find swift eager hands out-stretched in welcome.

I will seek Beauty all my days, and in my quest
    I shall not be dismayed.

    I SHALL FIND GOD

Minnie Aumonier

17 God

That unspeakable mystery which we worship
and which is everywhere whole and invisibly
    present
Father, Son and Holy Spirit,
One essence, undivided Majesty,
Splendour beyond all radiances and glory beyond all
    praise.
This the perfectly pure mind wholly surrendered to
    God may in some manner perceive, but not
    adequately explain:
For how should it be possible to speak comprehen-
    sively of him who cannot be grasped by the mind
    of a creature?

Cassiodorus c. 485 - c. 580

18 God

If the thought ever comes to you that everything that
you have thought about God is mistaken and that there

is no God, do not be dismayed. It happens to many people. But do not think that the source of your unbelief is that there is no God. If you no longer believe in the God in whom you believed before, this comes from the fact that there was something wrong with your belief, and you must strive to understand better that which you call God. When a savage ceases to believe in his wooden God, that does not mean that there is no God, but only that the true God is not of wood.

Leo Tolstoy 1828 - 1910

19 God

May the strength of God pilot us.
May the power of God preserve us.
May the wisdom of God instruct us.
May the hand of God protect us.
May the way of God direct us.
May the shield of God defend us.
May the host of God guard us against the snares
    of evil and the temptations of the world.
May Christ be with us.
    Christ before us.
    Christ in us.
    Christ over us.
May thy salvation, O Lord, be always ours
    this day and for evermore. Amen.

St Patrick 389 - 461

20 God

What a joy and happiness it is to be quite sure that there is a God ... something infinitely more real than the air

around us, and the flight of the birds, and the trials ...
and needs of our little lives. The reality, one and har-
monious, strong and self-sufficing, God.

Friedrich von Hügel 1852 - 1925

21 | God

There is nothing quite so exquisite as the shadow of
God in the desert.

Cesar Jerez SJ

22 | God

Oh Thou who art!
Ecclesiastes names thee Almighty,
Maccabees names thee Creator;
the Epistle to the Ephesians names thee Liberty;
Baruch names thee Immensity;
the Psalms name thee Wisdom and Truth;
John names thee Light;
the Book of Kings names thee Lord;
Exodus calls thee Providence;
Leviticus, Holiness;
Esdras, Justice;
Creation calls thee God;
Man names thee Father;
but Solomon names thee Compassion,
and that is the most beautiful of all thy names.

Victor Hugo 1802 - 1885

23 | God's plan

One of the challenges we all face is to be continually sensitive to the unfolding of God's plan in our lives; to give free and open assent to the destiny his love is shaping for us.

It is so easy to lose that sensitivity. So much of our life is dominated by the mechanical, by the response that is expected or demanded of us, by attempts to predict or anticipate growth, that we are always in danger of losing contact with life as a mystery and so with life itself.

Any fixed pattern we try to impose on our life falsifies the truth of the mystery that is eternally present and so unpredictable.

Our day-to-day life is of vital importance as the mystery of transformation is worked out in us and through us by the power of Christ. No detail is insignificant because the reassimilation of all creation in Christ is to be complete.

The plan being worked out in the life of each of us is the same as that being realized in all creation, the bringing into unity with Christ of all that is. The first sphere of this great movement into unity is the achievement of wholeness within ourselves.

John Main OSB 1926 - 1986

24 | Goodness

Thy goodness transcends my power to recount it in words. A hundred thousand years are not enough to tell the story of thy infinite goodness, O ineffable Lord. Words are but feeble expressions of the grateful feelings that fill my heart and soul. I thank thee on my knees with my whole soul, O Lord of goodness.

When I recall the countless benefits of life that thou, in thy manifold goodness, dost confer upon me, my heart glows with devotion for thee. Let goodness be a part of my being, my nature. Let it grow in me from day to day. Let my goodness be the habitual and instinctive. Let me think goodness, speak goodness and do goodness. Let me hunger and thirst after goodness.

Help me to be good, but help me, my heavenly Father, to make others good. Help me to play my part, however humble, in the direction of doing good and diffusion of goodness. Let my prayer in deeds of goodness to others ever follow my prayer in words to thee.

Zoroastrian Yasna

25 | Government

When it shall be said in any country in the world, "My poor are happy; neither ignorance nor distress is to be found among them; my jails are empty of prisoners, my streets of beggars; the aged are not in want, the taxes are not oppressive..." – when these things can be said, then may that country boast of its constitution and government.

Thomas Paine 1737 - 1809

26 | Grace

The Lord sees your need and your efforts, and will give you a helping hand. He will support and establish you as a soldier, fully armed and ready to go into battle. No support can be better than his. The greatest danger lies in the soul thinking that it can find this help within itself; then it will lose everything. Evil will dominate it again, eclipsing the light that as yet flickers but weakly in the soul, and it will extinguish the small flame which is still scarcely burning. The soul should realise how powerless it is alone; therefore, expecting nothing of itself, let it fall down in humility before God, and in its own heart recognise itself to be nothing. Then grace – which is all powerful – will, out of this nothingness, create in it everything. He who in total humility puts himself in the hands of the merciful God, attracts the Lord to himself, and becomes strong in his strength.

Although expecting everything from God and nothing from ourselves, we must nevertheless force ourselves to action, exerting all our strength, so as to create something to which the divine help may come, and which the divine power may encompass. Grace is always present within us, but it will only act after man himself has acted, filling his powerlessness with its own power. Establish yourself, therefore, firmly in the humble sacrifice of your will to God and then take action without any irresolution or half-heartedness.

The Art of Prayer – an Orthodox anthology

27 | Gratitude

The world is mine!

Today upon a bus I saw a lovely girl with golden
    hair;
I envied her ... she seemed so gay ... and wished I
    were as fair.
When suddenly she rose to leave, I saw her hobble
    down the aisle;
She had one foot and wore a crutch, but as she
    passed a smile.

Oh God, forgive me when I whine;
I have two feet ... the world is mine!

And then I stopped to buy some sweets.
The lad who served them had such charm, I talked
    with him.
He said to me: "It's nice to talk to folks like you.
You see," he said, "I'm blind."

Oh, God forgive me when I whine;
I have two eyes ... the world is mine!

Then, walking down the street, I saw a child with
    eyes of blue.
He stood and watched the others play;
It seemed he knew not what to do.
I stopped for a moment, then I said, "Why don't you
    join the others, dear?"
He looked ahead without a word, and then I knew
    he could not hear.

Oh God, forgive me when I whine;
I have two ears ... and the world is mine!

With feet to take me where I'd go,
With eyes to see the sunset's glow,
With ears to hear what I would know,

Oh God, forgive me when I whine;
I'm blessed indeed! The world is mine!

Anon.

28 Gratitude

Lord Jesus Christ,
my merciful redeemer and my compassionate
    saviour.
I praise you and I give you thanks.
I know my thanks are quite inadequate for all the
kindness you have shown to me,

I know they lack the fervour that they ought
   to have,
and are a poor return for the abundance
of your tender love that I so much desired.
And yet my soul must pay its debt somehow.
I cannot praise and thank you as I ought;
but at least I will do the best I can.

St Anselm 1033 - 1109

29 | Grief

There is no grief which time does not lessen and soften.

Cicero 106 B.C. - 43 B.C.

30 | Handicapped, The

To my handicapped son

So many lessons you have taught,
Contradictions you have brought.

Your infirmities have shown
Blessed strengths that were unknown.

Have shown that joy can be disguised,
And come in ways not recognised.

We used to think your days were spent
In empty, sad, bewilderment.

No words to speak, no thoughts to give,
For what reason did you live?

We dwelt with sorrow, pain, despair,
And angry bitterness was there.

But love was there, a love that grew
In all the hearts that cherished you.

So strong a love, searching to find
What lay within your hidden mind.

A patient love, that, day by day,
Eased the barriers away.

To glimpse, at last, the light that played
Like broken sunbeams through dark shade.

We found your nature's gentleness,
Your heart, that holds no worldliness,

Your soul in innocence arrayed,
Detached and tranquil, unafraid.

Such loving trust, affection rare,
And true simplicity you bear.

To know such treasures you possess
Softens and heals our bitterness.

May God our questionings forgive,
We know, now, the reason why you live.

Patricia Davis

May

1 | Happiness

The heart is rich when it is content, and it is always content when its desires are fixed on God. Nothing can bring greater happiness than doing God's will for the love of God.

Blessed Miguel Febres Cordero-Munoz 1854 - 1910

2 | Happiness

They taught me that happiness could be simply attained. I could either do my duty in that station of life to which it has pleased God to call me: or I could take evening classes in book-keeping and go one better than he intended!

Aubrey Menen

3 | Healing

To be persons, in the Christian sense, means that we must bear one another's burdens. We must be prepared to suffer pain for one another and to carry each other in love through times of darkness and dread. We must take on what we can of each other's violence and woundedness without allowing ourselves the relief of retaliation. Only if we are prepared to do this do we enter the privilege of the Gospel, which is to heal each other and find our healing in and through each other.

Angela Tilby

4 Heaven

The gateway to perfect love

I say to my people who are dying: "Soon after you're dead – we're not sure how long – but not long you'll be united with the most ecstatic love you've ever known. As one of the best things in your life was human love, this will be love, but much more satisfying, and it will last FOREVER."

Cardinal Basil Hume OSB

5 Help

However perplexed you may at any hour become about some question of truth, one refuge and resource is always at hand: you can do something for someone besides yourself. When your own burden is heaviest, you can always lighten a little some other's burden. At the times when you cannot see God, there is still open to you this sacred possibility, to show God; for it is the love and kindness of human hearts through which the divine reality comes home to people, whether they name it or not. Let this thought, then, stay with you; there may be times when you cannot find help, but there is no time when you cannot give help.

George S. Merriam

6 Help unfailing

Lord,
I lift up my eyes
and see my own anxiety,

the worry that intrudes
no matter how I try to shut it out,
that haunts my day
and frets my sleep.
Lord,
from where does my help come?

This is not my first crisis,
nor will it be the last.
Time and again
I have met goblins of worry,
seen giant waves
rise up to engulf me.
Yet still
I have not been overwhelmed.
Hopes and fears,
dreams and disasters
litter my wake,
yet still I am here,
looking up once more to you.
For you are the one constant,
unchanging strength of my life.
When friends desert me,
you remain.
When my body fails,
you support me.
When my thoughts are in turmoil,
you bring peace.

"From whence does my help come?
My help comes from the Lord
who neither slumbers, nor sleeps,
the Lord who made heaven and earth."

"The Lord will keep you from all evil;
he will keep your life.
The Lord will keep
your going out and your coming in
from this time forth and for ever more."

Frank Topping

7 | Holiness

Our Lord has created persons for all states in life, and in all of them we see people who have achieved sanctity by fulfilling their obligations well.

St Anthony Mary Claret 1807 - 1880

8 | Holiness

There is no single definition of holiness: there are dozens, hundreds. But there is one I am particularly fond of: being holy means getting up immediately every time you fall, with humility and joy. It doesn't mean never falling into sin. It means being able to say, "Yes, Lord, I have fallen a thousand times. But thanks to you I have got up again a thousand and one times." That's all. I like thinking about that.

Archbishop Helder Camara

9 | Holiness

O God, our Father, we are helpless without your help.
Unless you help us,
We can see the ideal
but we cannot reach it.
We can know the right
but we cannot do it.
We can recognise our duty
but we cannot perform it.
We can seek the truth
but we can never wholly find it.
All our lives we are haunted by the difference

between what we ought to do and what in fact
we can do.
By your Holy Spirit,
enlighten our minds,
that we may reach beyond guessing to knowing,
and beyond doubt to certainty.
Purify our hearts,
that wrong desires may not only be kept under
control,
but may be completely taken away.
Strengthen our will,
that we may pass beyond resolving to doing,
and beyond intention to action.
O God, our Father, this day we rest our weakness in
your strength and our insufficiency in your completeness. Take us, and do for us what we cannot do, and
make us what we cannot be. Through Jesus Christ.

William Barclay 1907 - 1978

10 Holiness

He that sees the beauty of holiness, or true moral good
sees the greatest and most important thing in the world
... Unless this is seen nothing is seen that is worth
seeing: for there is no other true excellence or beauty.

Jonathan Edwards 1746

11 Holy Spirit

On your last days on earth
you promised
to leave us the Holy Spirit
as our present comforter.

We also know that your Holy Spirit blows over this
earth.
But we do not understand him.
Many think
he is only wind or a feeling.
Let your Holy Spirit
break into our lives.
Let him come like blood into our veins,
so that we will be driven entirely by your will.
Let your Spirit
blow over wealthy Europe and America,
so that men there will be humble.
Let him blow over the poor parts of the world,
so that men there need suffer no more.
Let him blow over Africa,
so that men here may understand what true
freedom is.
There are a thousand voices and spirits in this
world,
but we want to hear only your voice,
and be open only to your Spirit.

Prayer of a young Ghanaian Christian

12 Holy Spirit

In the hour of my distress,
When temptations me oppress,
And when I my sins confess,
　　Sweet Spirit comfort me!

When I lie within my bed,
Sick in heart and sick in head,
And with doubts discomforted,
　　Sweet Spirit comfort me!

When the house doth sigh and weep,
And the world is drowned in sleep,

Yet mine eyes the watch do keep,
   Sweet Spirit comfort me!

When the tapers now burn blue,
And the comforters are few,
And that number more than true,
   Sweet Spirit comfort me!

When the priest his last hath prayed,
And I nod to what is said,
Cause my speech is now decayed
   Sweet Spirit comfort me!

When (God knows) I'm tossed about,
Either with despair or doubt,
Yet before the glass be out,
   Sweet Spirit comfort me!

When the Tempter me pursu'th
With the sins of all my youth,
And half damns me with untruth,
   Sweet Spirit comfort me!

When the judgement is revealed,
And that opened which was sealed,
When to thee I have appealed,
   Sweet Spirit comfort me!

Robert Herrick 1591 - 1674
some verses from "His Litany to the Holy Spirit"

13 Hope

O God, we hope in you
that you will help us in all our troubles
that you will strengthen us in all our temptations
that you will forgive us all our sins
that you will be with us when we die
   and be merciful to us when we are judged.

O God in you have we trusted, let us never be confounded.

Nigerian Lenten prayer

14 | Hope

Hope looks for the good in people
  instead of harping on the worst.
Hope opens doors where despair closes them.
Hope discovers what can be done
  instead of grumbling about what cannot.
Hope draws its power from a deep trust in God
  and the basic goodness of mankind.
Hope "lights a candle," instead of cursing the darkness.
Hope regards problems small or large,
  as opportunities.
Hope pushes ahead when it would be easy to quit.
Hope puts up with modest gains,
  realizing that "the longest journey starts with
  one step."
Hope accepts misunderstanding
  as the price for serving the greater good of others.
Hope is a good loser
  because it has the divine assurance of final victory.

James Keller

15 | Hope

It's really a wonder that I haven't dropped all my ideals because they seem so absurd and impossible to carry out. Yet I still keep them because in spite of everything I still believe that people are really good at heart.

I simply cannot build my hopes on a foundation consisting of confusion, misery and death. I see the world gradually being turned into a wilderness. I hear the ever approaching thunder which will destroy us too. I can feel the sufferings of millions and yet when I look up into the heavens I think that it will all come right; that the cruelty too will end and that peace and tranquillity will return again.

In the meantime I must uphold my ideals for perhaps the time will come when I shall be able to carry them out.

Ann Frank 1929 - 1945

16 Hope

What then is the Christian hope, and how has it so radically altered my own attitude to dying as a young man of thirty-seven with a wife and two children whom I am leaving behind?

... I believe that there is no ground for fear of death and what comes after. The process of dying is one of which I do sometimes become fearful, and this is a natural reaction and one that was experienced, I believe, even by Our Lord himself in Gethsemane. But the freedom from fear of death itself is even more liberating when it is seen in the biblical context. Forgiveness lies in a personal acceptance of the death of Christ on our behalf, not by dying as a man might die for his country or his family, but as the Son of God, for a sinful person: that is, me. Once such a step has been taken, hope begins to take shape; and once the underlying truth of the resurrection has been understood, the real wonder of it all becomes crystal clear. This new life becomes ours, only a shadow now, but after death to go on for ever. The choice is ours. All the facts are available to us. God's judgement will be manifestly fair, most of all to those who are judged. This is not easy to accept, but I can promise each and every one who takes such a step of faith that any fear of death will go.

Dr James H. Casson 1943 - 1980

17 | Humanity

First they came for the Jews
and I did not speak out –
because I was not a Jew.

Then they came for the communists
and I did not speak out –
because I was not a communist.

Then they came for the trade unionists
and I did not speak out –
because I was not a trade unionist.

Then they came for me –
and there was no one left
to speak out for me.

Pastor Niemoeller 1892 - 1984

18 | Humility

Instead of wasting energy in being disgusted with
yourself, accept your own failure, and just say to God,
"Well, in spite of all I may say or fancy, this is what I
am really like – so please help my weakness." This, not
self-disgust, is the real and fruitful humility.

Evelyn Underhill 1875 - 1941

19 | Idols

If we idolize wealth, then we create poverty;
if we idolize success, we create the inadequate;
if we idolize power, we create powerlessness.
And these processes are inevitable.

Thomas Cullinan OSB

20 | Individuality

All of us are blessed with
individuality.
We're different from each other –
that's how God meant us to be.
So when opinions differ
and you don't see eye-to-eye
or angry words are spoken
and tempers start to fly
calm yourself and try to see
the other person's view.
Mediate your differences
as God wants you to do,
for by living well with others
through every kind of strife
our horizons broaden
and we get more from life!

21 | Individuality

Do not attempt to cast yourself into the mould
occupied
    by another,
for every mould is unique in structure and concept,
and only the person for whom it was cast, can
occupy
    that particular mould.
Individuality is God's gift to every person.
No-one exactly duplicates another, not even
"identical twins",
    for even they have
    separate personalities.

God created you
to fulfil a specific purpose in life.

He did not form you to slavishly imitate another.
Find the way in which you are directed,
   and follow it, and it alone.

Trust in the merciful, all-embracing love of God,
even when you stray from your own appointed path
in thought, deed, or in active participation in those
things
   which are abhorrent to your inner self.
Even then, God still loves you,
and wants you safe within his arms, once more.

Your path is not easy, no path reaching towards
heaven ever was, is, or will be –
But accept your daily journey,
   bewildering though it may appear.

Trust in God, and
   He will guide you
through the direction of those whom
he has appointed to serve, guide, and direct you
   with their wisdom and counsel.

Patricia Vardigans

22 | Jesus Christ

*The twenty-third Psalm for busy people
(A translation by a Japanese Christian)*

The Lord is my pacesetter, I shall not rush.
He makes me stop and rest for quiet intervals.
He provides me with images of stillness which restore
   my serenity.
He leads me in ways of efficiency through calmness of
   mind.
His guidance is peace.

Even though I have a great many things to accomplish
    each day,
I will not fret,
For his presence is here, his timelessness, his all
    importance will keep me in balance.
He prepares refreshment and renewal in the midst of
    my activity by anointing my mind with oils of
    tranquillity.
My cup of joyous energy overflows.
Such harmony and effectiveness shall be the fruit of my
    hours,
For I shall walk in the peace of the Lord and dwell in
    his house for ever.

Toki Miyashina

23 | Jesus Christ

Lord Jesus, let all that is you flow into me.
Let your body and blood be my food and my drink,
Your passion and death be my strength and my life.
Lord Jesus, with you at my side enough has been
    given.
May the shelter I seek be the shadow of your cross.
Let me not run from the love that you offer
but hold me safe against the forces of evil.
On each of my dyings shed your light and your
    love.
Keep calling me until that day comes when
with your saints I may praise you for ever.

A modern translation of the "Anima Christi"

24 | Jesus Christ

Jesus of Nazareth was the most scientific man that ever trod the globe. He plunged beneath the material surface of things, and found the spiritual cause.

Mary Baker Eddy 1821 - 1910

25 | Jesus Christ

(Jesus) a man who was innocent, offered himself as a sacrifice for the good of others, including his enemies, and became the ransom of the world. It was a perfect act.

Gandhi 1869 - 1948

26 | Jesus Christ

Lord, look for me among the bleakness of my heart.
Lord, look for me among the pain that tears my soul apart.
If you will find me, Lord,
while I am lost,
my senses muddled, hope abandoned,
into the dark I'm tossed.
Where is the road of freedom from despair –
the morning song I cannot hear?
If you will find me, Lord,
just take my trembling hand
and walk beside me, Lord,
my rescue and my friend.

Teresa Meadows

27 Jesus Christ

One solitary life

He was born in a stable,
In an obscure village,
the child of a peasant woman.
He worked in a carpenter's shop
until he was thirty.
From there he travelled,
Less than 200 miles.

He never wrote a book.
He never held office.
He never had a family or owned a home.
He did none of the things one
usually associates with greatness.

He became a nomadic preacher.
He was only thirty-three when the tide of
Popular opinion turned against him,
He was betrayed by a close friend,
And his other friends ran away.
He was turned over to his enemies
and went through the mockery of a trial.
He was unjustly condemned to death,
Crucified on a cross between two thieves,
On a hill overlooking the town dump,
And, when dead, was laid in a borrowed grave,
through the pity of a friend.

Nineteen centuries have come and gone,
all the armies that ever marched,
all the navies that ever sailed,
all the parliaments that ever sat,
and all the kings that ever reigned
have not affected the life of man on this earth
as that One Solitary Life.

He is the central figure of the human race,
He is the Messiah, the Son of God,
JESUS CHRIST.

28 Jesus Christ

Dear Friend,

I just had to send you a note to tell you how much I love and care about you. Yesterday, I saw you walking with your friends. I waited all day hoping you would want to talk with me. As evening drew near, I gave you a sunset to close your day and a cool breeze to rest you. Then I waited; but you never came. Yes, I was disappointed, but I still love you because you are my friend.

When you fell asleep last night, I longed to touch your brow, so I spilled moonlight on your pillow and face. Again I waited, wanting to rush down so that we could talk – I have so many gifts for you. But you awakened late the next day and rushed off to work ... My tears were in the rain.

Today you looked so sad, all alone. It makes my heart ache because I understand. My friends let me down so many times too, but I love you. Oh! if you would only listen to me. I really love you. I try to tell you in the blue sky and in the quiet green grass; I whisper it in the leaves on the trees and breathe it in the colour of the flowers. I shout it to you in the mountain streams and give the birds love songs to sing. I clothe you with warm sunshine and perfume the air with nature's scent. My love for you is deeper than the oceans and greater than any need you might have.

We will spend eternity together in heaven. I know how hard it is on this earth; I really know because I was there. If only you knew how much I want to help you. My Father wants to help you, too. He's that way, you know.

Just call upon me, ask me, talk to me. It is your decision. You are free to call me, it's up to you. I'll wait, since I have chosen you and will never leave you – because I love you.

Your friend,
Jesus

29 Jesus Christ

Thou shalt know him
When he comes
Not by any din of drums
Nor the vantage of his airs
Nor by anything he wears
Neither by his crown
Nor his gown
For his presence known shall be
By the holy harmony
That his coming makes in me.

Anon. c. 1500

30 Jesus Christ

He gave us a vision of God
where others could only speak of it.

31 Jesus Christ

Dearest Lord, may I see you today and every day in the person of your sick, and whilst nursing them minister unto you.

Though you hide yourself behind the unattractive disguise of the irritable, the exacting, the unreasonable, may I still recognise you and say: "Jesus, my patient, how sweet it is to serve you."

Lord, give me this seeing faith, then my work will never be monotonous. I will ever find joy in humouring the fancies and gratifying the wishes of all poor sufferers.

O beloved sick, how doubly dear you are to me, when you personify Christ; and what a privilege is mine to be allowed to tend you.

Sweetest Lord, make me appreciative of the dignity of my high vocation, and its many responsibilities. Never permit me to disgrace it by giving way to coolness, unkindness, or impatience.

And, O God, while you are Jesus, my patient, deign also to be to me a patient Jesus, bearing with my faults, looking only to my intention, which is to love and serve you in the person of each of your sick.

Lord, increase my faith, bless my efforts and work, now and for evermore.

Prayer said by Mother Teresa of Calcutta each day

1 Jesus Christ

No book on theology or ethics, no matter how inspired, can fill the immense gap between our finiteness and the undreamed-of greatness of God. Only Jesus closed the gap, but starting from the other end, by stripping off his divine majesty and putting on our human existence. Only he was able to know ever when to resist and when to surrender. Moreover, this demanded of him the utmost faithfulness in meditation, in fasting, in prayer. This is why Christianity is not so much a body of principles as it is a commitment to his person. By him, in fellowship with him, it is possible for us to receive certain benefits of grace, a few rays of light far more authentic and trustworthy than the whole store of human knowledge

All we can do is try: try sincerely to live a life guided by God. If we want to be altogether sure of his guidance before beginning, we shall fall back into all the problems we have already described. He who does not dare risk being mistaken about the will of God will never come to know him any better. For it is through obedience, yes, even through our misguided actions, that we find even greater light. That is, on condition that we are willing to re-examine our actions afterwards quite honestly and as in the presence of God. God is ever the hidden one who reveals himself only through our groping after him.

Paul Tournier 1905 - 1986

2 Jesus Christ

Jesus was there, when you prayed last night,
He talked with God, about you.
Jesus was there, when you fought that fight,
He is going to see you through.

Jesus knew when you shed those tears.
You did not weep alone,
For the burden you thought too heavy to bear,
He made his very own.
Jesus himself was touched by that trial,
Which you could not understand.
Jesus stood by as you almost fell,
And lovingly grasped your hand.
Jesus cared when you bore that pain,
Indeed, he bore it too.
He felt each pang, and ache in your heart,
Because of his love for you.
Jesus was grieved when you doubted his love,
But he gave you the grace to go on.
Jesus rejoiced when you trusted him,
The only trustworthy one.
His presence shall ever be near you,
No need to be anxious or fret,
Dear wonderful Lord, he was there all the time,
He has never forsaken you yet.

3 | Jesus Christ

Jesus, my Lord,
Come to me,
Comfort me, console me.
Visit the hearts
In strange lands
Yearning for you.
Visit the dying and those
Who have died without you.
Jesus, my Lord,
Visit also those
Who persecute you.
Lord Jesus, you are my light
In the darkness.

You are my warmth
In the cold.
You are my happiness
In sorrow ...

Anon.

4 Jesus Christ

Where would we be without Christ our Lord?
We would be lost and walking in darkness
He is the lantern that lights up that darkness
and he is the shepherd who finds the right path.

Chorus: So let the trumpet sound to the glory of
God.
He is our Lord, loving and wise.

Where would we be without Christ our Lord?
We would be left to wander the desert.
He is the beacon that leads us to safety,
and he is the water that brings us new life.

Where would we be without Christ our Lord?
We would be cold and starving and thirsty.
He is the bread that is food for the spirit,
and he is the wine of the new covenant.

Where would we be without Christ our Lord?
He is the Son who saves all the nations.
Through Christ the Son we are given the Spirit,
and this is the Spirit who brings us new life.

Chorus: So let the trumpet sound to the glory of
God.
He is our Lord, loving and wise.

Michael Cockett

5 | Jesus Christ

With him and nothing else you can be happy but without him and with all else you'll never be happy.

Patrick Henry

6 | Jesus Christ

I praise him most, I love him best, all praise and
  love is his;
While him I love, in him I live, and cannot live
  amiss.
Love's sweetest mark, laud's highest theme, man's
  most desired light,
To love him life, to leave him death, to live in him
  delight.
He mine by gift, I his by debt, thus to each other
  due,
First Friend He was, best Friend he is, all times will
  try him true;
His knowledge rules, his strength defends, his love
  doth cherish all;
His birth our joy, his life our light, his death our end
  of thrall.

Robert Southwell 1561? - 1595

7 | Jesus Christ

A God who empties himself and becomes a slave, who
endures mockery and humiliating death, and yet is
raised from the dead in glory, exposes the lie, the real
madness, of living only for self: God's ecstasy-in-Incarnation, his leaping down from heaven, demonstrates
once and for all that self-preservation leads to death

while self-oblation leads to eternal life. The Gospel of "an incarnate God, a God put to death", disrupts and subverts the worldly mind, shows it up for the madness it is.

John Saward

8 Joy

Into all our lives, in many simple, familiar, homely ways, God infuses this element of joy from the surprises of life, which unexpectedly brighten our days, and fill our eyes with light ... The success we were not counting on, the blessing we were not trying after, the strain of music in the midst of drudgery, the beautiful morning picture or sunset glory thrown in as we pass to or from our daily business, the unsought word of encourage-ment or expression of sympathy, the sentence that meant for us more than the writer or speaker thought – these and a hundred others that everyone's experience can supply are instances of what I mean. You may call it accident or chance – it often is;
    you may call it human goodness – it often is;
        but always, always call it God's love
            for that is always in it.
These are the overflowing riches of his grace,
        these are his free gifts.

Samuel Longfellow 1819 - 1892

9 Judgement

Before I stand in judgement

Pray, don't find fault with the man who limps
or stumbles along the road,

94

Unless you have worn the shoes he wears –
or struggled beneath the load.
There may be tacks in his shoes that hurt,
though hidden away from view.
For the burden *he* bears – placed upon *your* back,
might cause you to stumble too.

Don't be harsh with the man who sins,
or pelt with words or stones
unless you are sure – yes doubly sure,
that you have no sins of your own.
For you know perhaps that the tempter's voice
should whisper as soft to you
As it did to him when he went astray
and would cause you to stagger too.

Don't sneer at the man who's down today,
unless you have felt the blow
That caused his fall – or felt the shame –
that only the fallen know.
You may be strong – but still the blows
that were his – if dealt to you
In the self same way – at the self same time
might cause you to stagger too.

10 Judgement

Judgement is whispering into the ear of a merciful and compassionate God the story of my life which I had never been able to tell.

Quoted by Cardinal Hume in his book To be a pilgrim

11 | Judgement

He who shall pass judgement on the records of our life is the same that formed us in frailty.

Robert L. Stevenson 1850 - 1894

12 | Kindness

Be kind and merciful. Let no one ever come to you without coming away better and happier. Be the living expression of God's kindness: kindness in your face, kindness in your eyes, kindness in your smile, kindness in your warm greeting. In the slums we are the light of God's kindness to the poor. To children, to the poor, to all who suffer and are lonely, give always a happy smile –
Give them not only your care, but also your heart.

Mother Teresa of Calcutta

13 | Kindness

Man cannot be too gentle, too kind. Shun even to appear harsh in your treatment of each other. But remember, no work of kindness or charity can bring down to earth the Holy Breath, unless it is done in the name of Christ. When it is, joy, radiant joy, streams from the face of him who gives and kindles joy in the heart of him who receives.

All condemnation is of the devil. Never condemn each other. Not even those you catch in the evil deed. We condemn each other only because we shun knowing ourselves. When we gaze at our own failings, we see such a morass of filth that nothing in another can equal it. That is why we turn away and make much of the faults of others. Keep away from the spilling of speech. Instead of condemning others, strive to reach the inner peace. Keep silent. Refrain from judgement. This will raise you above the deadly arrows of slander, insult, outrage – and will shield your glowing hearts against the evil that creeps around.

St Seraphim of Sarov 1759 - 1833

14 | Knowledge

Knowledge of God without knowing our own poverty makes for pride.

Knowledge of our own poverty without knowing God makes for despair.

Knowledge of Jesus Christ lets us be present both to God and to our poverty.

Blaise Pascal 1623 - 1662

15 | Life

Desiderata

Go placidly amid the noise and haste, and remember what peace there may be in silence. As far as possible without surrender be on good terms with all persons. Speak your truth quietly and clearly; and listen to others, even the dull and ignorant; they too have their story.

Avoid loud and aggressive persons, they are vexations to the spirit. If you compare yourself with others, you may become vain and bitter; for always there will be greater and lesser persons than yourself. Enjoy your achievements as well as your plans.

Keep interested in your own career, however humble; it is a real possession in the changing fortunes of time. Exercise caution in your business affairs; for the world is full of trickery. But let this not blind you to what virtue there is; many persons strive for high ideals; and everywhere life is full of heroism.

Be yourself. Especially, do not feign affection. Neither be cynical about love; for in the face of all aridity and disenchantment it is perennial as the grass.

Take kindly the counsel of the years, gracefully surrendering the things of youth. Nurture strength of spirit to shield you in sudden misfortune. But do not distress yourself with imaginings. Many fears are born of fatigue and loneliness. Beyond a wholesome discipline, be gentle with yourself.

You are a child of the universe, no less than the trees and the stars; you have a right to be here. And whether or not it is clear to you, no doubt the universe is unfolding as it should.

Therefore be at peace with God, whatever you conceive him to be, and whatever your labours and aspirations, in the noisy confusion of life keep peace with your soul.

With all its sham, drudgery and broken dreams, it is still a beautiful world. Be careful. Strive to be happy.

Found in Old St Paul's Church, Baltimore, U.S.A. 1692

16 | Life

My life and yours

To be glad of life because it gives you the chance to love and to work and to play and to look up at the stars, to be satisfied with your possessions but not contented with yourself until you have made the best of them; to despise nothing in the world except falsehood and meanness and to fear nothing except cowardice; to be governed by your admirations rather than your disgusts, to covet nothing that is your neighbour's except his kindness of heart and gentleness of manners, to think seldom of your enemies, often of your friends and every day of Christ and to spend as much time as you can with body and with spirit in God's out-of-doors. These are the little guide posts on the way to peace.

17 | Life

The good life exists only when you stop wanting a better one. It is the condition of savouring what is, rather than longing for what might be.

Marya Mannes

18 | Life

Live all you can; it's a mistake not to. It doesn't matter so much what you do in particular, so long as you have had your life. If you haven't had that, what have you had? What one loses one loses; make no mistake about that. The right time is any time that one is still lucky enough to be alive. Live!

Henry James 1843 - 1916

19 Life

Reasons for life

I don't know how to say it, but somehow it seems to
  me
That maybe we are stationed where God wants us to
  be;
That the little place I'm filling is the reason for my
  birth,
And just to do the work I do, he sent me down on
  earth.
If God had wanted otherwise, I reckon he'd have
  made
Me just a little different, of a worse or better grade;
And, since God knows and understands all things of
  land and sea,
I fancy that he placed me here, just where he
  wanted me.
Sometimes, I get to thinking, as my labours I review,
That I should like a higher place with greater things
  to do;
But I come to the conclusion, when the envying is
  stilled,
That the post to which God sent me is the post he
  wanted filled.
So, I plod along and struggle in the hope, when day
  is through
That I'm really necessary to the things God wants to
  do;
And there isn't any service I can give, which I
  should scorn,
For it may be just the reason God allowed that I be
  born.

20 | Life

Let me do my work each day; and if the darkened hours of despair overcome me, may I not forget the strength that comforted me in the desolation of other times. May I still remember the bright hours that found me walking over the silent hills of my childhood, or dreaming on the margin of the quiet river, when a light glowed within me and I promised my early God to have courage amid the tempests of the changing years.

Spare me from bitterness and from the sharp passions of unguarded moments. May I not forget that poverty and riches are of the spirit. Though the world know me not, may my thoughts and actions be such as shall keep me friendly with myself.

Lift my eyes from the earth, and let me not forget the use of the stars. Forbid that I should judge others, lest I condemn myself.

Let me not follow the clamour of the world, but walk calmly in my path. Give me a few friends who will love me for what I am; and keep ever burning before my vagrant eyes the kindly light of hope. Though age and infirmity overtake me, and I come not within sight of the castle of my dreams, teach me still to be thankful for life, and for time's golden memories that are good and sweet; and may the evening's twilight find me gentle still.

Max Ehrmann 1872 - 1945

21 | Life

Just to be is a blessing.
  Just to live is holy.

Abraham Heschel 1907 - 1972

22 | Life

Life is a movement, evolution, progression and not stagnation; it can be comprehended only in its incessant becoming, in its total continuity. You need a sense of history if you are to make sense of life. If you look only at the point where you are, you will see neither where you came from nor where you are going. One of the dimensions of your consciousness as a living being is missing if you do not enter into relationship with all age-groups, and more particularly with those who are nearing the end of their lives.

Paul Tournier 1905 - 1986

23 | Life

Lord of my origin
Draw me closer to you
Lord of my existence
Direct all my ways
Lord of my calling
Give me strength to go on
Lord of my faith
Preserve me from doubt
Lord of my hope
Keep me from despair
Lord of my love
Let me never grow cold
Lord of my past
May I never forget you
Lord of my present
Be near me always
Lord of my future
Keep me faithful to the end
Lord of my life

Let me live in your presence
Lord of my death
Receive me at last
Lord of my eternity
Bless me forever. Amen.

Eric Doyle OFM 1938 - 1986

24 | Life

The most solid barriers are not made of steel but of hard
and cruel hearts, which have no pity, not to mention
love for those who suffer. It is here (in prison) that one
realises that it is not where we live but how we live that
is important.

Frantisck Lizna SJ

25 | Life

Be in love with life,
Wrestle with the chaos and the pain, yourself and
    others, spirit echoing spirit.
Trusting in the victory of the vulnerable,
Glimpsing the peace, the wholeness, the
    spaciousness and the joy
That come from following the Pioneer, made perfect
    in suffering
Striving and yearning and crying out from the depths
    and heights of the world's anguish, and its bliss
So becoming friends and partners of God in the
    divine creating.

N. Kazanteakiz

26 | Life

Life breaks all of us sometimes,
    but some grow strong at broken places.

Ernest Hemingway 1898 - 1961

27 | Listening

Listen to yourself, so as to find the path to God
    within the frail walls of your humanness,
Listen to yourself, for it is you alone who will lead
    yourself to him, or away from him.
Listen to yourself, listen to God, when you have led
    yourself to him.
Listen, well, for if you hear his voice
you will be wise with the wisdom of the Lord,
and then you will be able to hear the voice of men,
not as a surging sea, or as a mob.
But each man's speech is his own,
a treasure given to you beyond all expectations,
because you led yourself to him and listened to his
voice.

Catherine de Hueck Doherty 1900 -

28 | Love

You loved us first so that we might love you. And this
was not because you needed to be loved by us, but
because we could not be what you created us to be
unless we loved you.

William of St-Thierry c. 1085 - 1148

29 | Love

Love, they say, is patient,
Love, they say, is kind.
It sees beyond another's faults
for love, they say, is blind.

Love takes away the me and mine,
Instead it's us and we.
Yours and mine is ours now
For love is unity.

Love will not diminish
Or rust or fade with years.
But it will gain its strength
from time, from laughter, joy and tears.

Love is God's own gift to us,
A present from above.
He gives us peace, he gives us joy,
But first he gives us love.

30 | Love

On this day ... Mend a quarrel ... Search out a forgotten
friend ... Dismiss suspicion, and replace it with trust ...
Write a love letter ... Share some treasure ... Give a soft
answer ... Encourage youth ... Manifest your loyalty in
a word or deed ... Keep a promise ... Find the time ...
Forego a grudge ... Forgive an enemy ... Listen ...
Apologise if you were wrong ... Try to understand ...
Flout envy ... Examine your demands on others ...
Think first of someone else ... Appreciate, be kind, be
gentle ... Laugh a little more ... Deserve confidence ...
Take up arms against malice ... Decry complacency ...
Express your gratitude ... Worship your God ... Glad-
den the heart of a child ... Take pleasure in the beauty
and wonder of the earth ... Speak your love ... Speak
it again ... Speak it still again ... speak it still once again.

July

1 Love

To renounce your individuality, to see with another's eyes, to hear with another's ears, to be two and yet be one, to so melt and mingle that you no longer know you are you, to constantly absorb and constantly radiate, to reduce earth, sea and sky and all that is in them to a single being, to give yourself to that being so wholly that nothing whatever is withheld, to be prepared at any moment for sacrifice, to double your personality in bestowing it: that is love.

Theophile Gautier 1811 - 1872

2 Love

There is nothing you can do for Christ that will give him greater pleasure than that you believe in his love, his unconditional love for you. You will probably find that doing that is more difficult than some of the generous sacrifices you were planning to make, and that it brings infinitely greater spiritual joy and spiritual progress than all the things you do for Christ.

Anthony de Mello SJ

3 Love

Take, O Lord, and receive
All my liberty, my memory, my understanding
And all my will,
Whatever I have or possess.
You have given all these things to me.
To you, O Lord, I restore them.

They are yours,
Dispose of them according to your will.
Give me your love and your grace
For this is enough for me.

St Ignatius of Loyola 1495 - 1556

4 | Love

We hold in your presence, O Lord,
all those we love and those who love us.
Your love is so much greater than ours
and you work unceasingly for our well-being,
With all the resources of infinite wisdom and
    patience.
Bestow on them the fullness of your blessing.

Heavenly Father, give me a genuine love for others,
both those I like and those I don't like;
help me to overcome my fears and prejudices
and to see your image in all men.

O Christ who welcome the downtrodden,
those made to feel small,
help us to enlarge others rather than diminish them;
to build up rather than to belittle.

Bishop Richard Harries

5 | Love

Love is the greatest thing that God can give us, for
himself is Love; and it is the greatest thing we can give
to God, for it will also give ourselves, and carry with it
all that is ours. The Apostle calls it, *the bond of perfection*; it is the Old, and it is the New, and it is the great
Commandment, and it is all the Commandments, for it
is *the fulfilling of the law*. It does the work of all other

graces, without any instrument but its own immediate virtue... It is a grace that loves God for himself, and our neighbour for God. The consideration of God's goodness and bounty, the experience of those profitable and excellent emanations from him, may be, and most commonly are, the first motive of our love: but when we are once entered, and have tasted the goodness of God, we love the spring for its own excellency, passing from passion to reason, from thinking to adoring, from sense to spirit, from considering our selves to a union with God: and this is the image and little representation of Heaven; it is beatitude, in pictures, or rather the infancy and beginnings of glory.

Jeremy Taylor 1613 - 1667
Holy Living: of Charity,
or the Love of God, *1650*

Lord William Rees Mogg comments on this piece: When one has read that passage one should pause, and if possible read it again, for it sums up not only the central doctrine of the Christian faith, but the central truth about the religious nature of man. It is the message of the Gospels: it is the message of Jesus; it is put with the most beautiful eloquence by St Paul. It is the truth by which the saints were changed and it is the truth for which martyrs died, but it is also the great and general consolation of mankind.

6 | Love

Love has also the power of transforming, for it transforms the lover into his Beloved, and makes him dwell in him. Thus it happens that when the fire of the Holy Spirit really gets hold of the heart, it sets it wholly on fire, and, so to speak, turns it into a flame, leading into that state in which it is most like God.

Richard Rolle c. 1300 - 1349

7 | Love

Nothing in life is happier than to love faithfully
– and to be loved in return.

Adam of Perseigne, 12th century

8 | Love of God

St Paul says that "All things work together for good to
them that love God..." First of all, the Apostle says, "all
things". He excepts nothing. All the events of Providence, whether fortunate or unfortunate, everything
that has to do with health, or wealth, or reputation;
every condition of life; all the different interior states
through which we may have to pass – desolation, dryness, disgust, weariness, temptations, all this to be for
the advantage of those who love God; and more than
this, even our faults, even our sins. – We must be
resolved never to offend God wilfully; but if unfortu-
nately we do offend him, our very offences, our very
crimes may be made use of for our advantage, if we
really love God. We have only to remember David, we
have only to remember St Peter, whose sins only served
to make them more holy afterwards, that is to say, more
humble, more grateful to God, more full of love... But
all these Divine arrangements are only good for those
who love God, that is to say, for those whose will is
united and submissive to the will of God – those who
in his service consider before all things the interests of
God, the glory of God, and the accomplishment of his
good pleasure – who are ready to sacrifice to him
everything without exception, and who are persuaded
that there is nothing better for a creature than to be lost
in God and for God, because it is the only means of
finding one's self again in him: for all this is loving God
truly, and with one's whole heart.

Jean Nicholas Grou SJ 1731 - 1803

9 | Love of God

Since he is wise he loves you with wisdom.
Since he is good he loves you with goodness.
Since he is holy he loves you with holiness.
Since he is just he loves you with justice.
Since he is merciful he loves you with mercy.
Since he is compassionate he loves you with compassion.
Since he is gentle he loves you with gentleness.

St John of the Cross 1542 - 1591

10 | Marriage

The art of marriage

A good marriage must be created.
In the marriage, the little things are the big things...
It is never being too old to hold hands.
It is remembering to say "I love you" at least once
each day.
It is never going to sleep angry.
It is having a mutual sense of values and common
objectives.
It is standing together and facing the world.
It is forming a circle of love that gathers in the
whole family.
It is speaking words of appreciation and
demonstrating gratitude in thoughtful ways.
It is having the capacity to forgive and forget.
It is giving each other an atmosphere in which each
can grow.
It is a common search for the good and the
beautiful.
It is not only marrying the right person,
It is being the right partner.

11 | Marriage

It hasn't been easy, Lord

It's twenty years, Lord.
Yes, twenty years since we were married.
It hasn't been easy, but Lord,
with your help we've made it.

We've had some rough times and shed
many tears, but Lord, we've also shared
a great deal of laughter together.
Please, Lord, give us many more years
to share together on this earth.

Lord, when it's time for one of us to part,
comfort the one that is left, until we can
walk together again in your beautiful garden.

Patricia W. Thompson

12 | Marriage

On their 50th wedding anniversary, a couple were asked
to sum up the reasons for their long and happy marriage.

The husband said: "I have never tried to be selfish. After
all, there is no 'I' in the word 'marriage'."

The wife added: "For my part, I have never corrected
my husband's spelling!"

13 | Mary

She is given to us as a pledge and guarantee that God's
plan in Christ for the salvation of the whole person has

already achieved realisation in a creature; in her.
Contemplated in the episodes of the Gospels and in the
reality which she already possesses in the City of God,
the Blessed Virgin Mary offers a calm vision and a
reassuring word to people of today, torn as they often
are between anguish and hope; defeated by the sense
of their own limitations and assailed by limitless aspirations, troubled in their minds and divided in their
hearts, uncertain before the riddle of death, oppressed
by loneliness while yearning for fellowship, a prey to
boredom and disgust. She shows forth the victory of
hope over anguish, of fellowship over loneliness, of
peace over anxiety, of joy and beauty over boredom
and disgust, of eternal visions over earthly ones, of life
over death.

Pope John Paul II
from the Encyclical 'Mother of the Redeemer'

14 Mary

There is actually only one person in all humanity of
whom God has one picture, and in whom there is a
perfect conformity between what he wanted her to be
and what she is – and that is his own Mother.

Anon.

15 Mary

The Blessed Virgin, by becoming the Mother of God,
received a kind of infinite dignity because God is infinite;
this dignity therefore is such a reality that a better is not
possible, just as nothing can be better than God.

St Thomas Aquinas 1225 - 1274

112

16 | Mary

Her highest privilege is her poverty, and her greatest glory is that she is most hidden, and the source of all her power is that she is as nothing in the presence of Christ.

Anon.

17 | Mary

The Blessed Virgin has ascended on high, and therefore she too will give gifts to human beings. And why not? Surely neither the ability nor the will to do so is lacking to her. She is Queen of heaven; she is compassionate; finally, she is the Mother of the only begotten Son.

St Bernard 1090 - 1153

18 | Mary

The Memorare

Remember, O most gracious Virgin Mary, that never was it known that anyone who fled to thy protection, implored thy help or sought thy intercession was left unaided. Inspired with this confidence, I fly unto thee. O Virgin of Virgins, my Mother. To thee I come, before thee I stand sinful and sorrowful. O Mother of the Word Incarnate, despise not my petitions, but in thy mercy hear and answer them, through Christ our Lord. Amen.

St Bernard 1090 - 1153

19 | Mary

O Mother of Sorrows,
With strength from above
You stood by the cross, sharing
In the sufferings of Jesus
And with tender care you bore him
In your arms, mourning and weeping.

We praise you for your faith
Which accepted the life God
Planned for you.

We praise you for your hope
Which trusted that he would do
Great things through you.

We praise you for your love
In bearing, with Jesus, the sorrows
Of his passion.

Holy Mary, may we follow your
Example and stand by all your
Children who need comfort and love.

Mother of God, stand by us in our
Trials and care for us in our many needs.
Pray for us now and at the hour of our
    death. Amen.

20 | Mary

The modern woman will note with pleasant surprise
that Mary of Nazareth ... was far from being a timidly
submissive woman. On the contrary, she was a woman
who did not hesitate to proclaim that God vindicates
the humble and oppressed and removes the powerful
people of the world from their privileged positions.

Pope Paul VI 1897 - 1978

21 | Mass, The

Whenever I celebrate Mass, I am always aware of doing something greater than myself, something greater than the simple actions involved, something greater than the Church and the world itself.

Mgr George A. Tomlinson 1906 - 1985

22 | Meditation

The great grace that all of us have been given is to believe in Jesus Christ, to believe in his presence in our hearts and to believe that he invites each of us to enter into that presence. That is an extraordinary gift to have been given.

We have to learn, because it is a gift of such staggering proportions, to respond to it gradually, gently. When we begin we cannot fully understand the sheer magnificence and wonder of it. Each time we return to meditate we enter into that reality a little more deeply, a little more faithfully.

When we begin we probably find our way to meditation as one among many options that we have been looking at and it takes us time to find that this is the pearl of great price.

I do not wish to imply that meditation is the only way, but rather that it is the only way I have found. In my experience it is the way of pure simplicity that enables us to become fully, integrally aware of the Spirit Jesus has sent into our heart. This is the recorded experience of the mainstream of the Christian tradition from apostolic times down to our own day.

John Main OSB 1926 -1986

23 Mercy

Beware, daughters, of a certain kind of humility suggested by the devil which is accompanied by great anxiety about the gravity of our sins.

He disturbs souls in many ways by this means, until at last he stops them from receiving Holy Communion and from private prayer by doubts as to whether they are in a fit state for it, and such thoughts as: "Am I worthy of it? Am I in a good disposition?"

Thus Christians are hindered from prayer, and when they communicate, the time during which they ought to be obtaining graces is spent in wondering whether they are well prepared or no.

Everything such a person says seems to her on the verge of evil, and all her actions appear fruitless, however good they are in themselves. She becomes discouraged and unable to do any good, for what is right in others she fancies wrong in herself.

When you are in this state, turn your mind so far as you can from your misery and fix it on the mercy of God, his love for us, and all that he suffered for our sake.

St Teresa of Avila 1515 - 1582

24 Mercy

The truth is that I am far from being the person I ought to be.
My life is a whole mess and tangle of subterfuges to evade grace and duty.

I have done all things badly,
I have thrown away great opportunities.

But my infidelity to Christ,
instead of making me sick with despair,
drives me to throw myself, all the more blindly,
into the arms of his mercy.

Thomas Merton 1915 - 1968

25 Mercy

The sinner of today is the saint of tomorrow. Wherefore, unmindful of the sins and shortcomings of our neighbour, let us look to our own imperfections, surely forgetting what God has forgotten: sins truly repented, which God has forgotten, 'tis no business of ours to remember.

Meister Eckhart 1260 - 1329

26 Money

Money cannot buy everything we need.
Money can buy a home but not a homeland.
Money can buy a wife but not children.
Money can buy a bed but not sleep.
Money can buy food but not appetite.
Money can buy medicine but not health.
Money can buy cosmetics but not beauty.
Money can buy books but not knowledge.
Money can buy luxury but not happiness.
Money can buy a car but not safe driving.
Money can buy friendship but not love.

T. Johnny

27 | Morning prayer

O my God, you love me,
You're with me night and day.
I want to love you always.
In all I do and say
I'll try to please you, Father.
Bless me through the day.

I thank you for the gift of being alive this morning,
I thank you for the sleep which has refreshed me,
I thank you for the chance to begin life all over
    again.

Lord, this day is full of promise and opportunity
Help me to waste none of it.
This day is full of mystery, and the unknown
Help me to face it without fear, and anxiety.
This day is full of adventure
Help me to be fully alive to it all.

During this day may I become
A more thoughtful person,
A more prayerful person,
A more generous and kindly person.
Help me not to be turned in on myself
But to be sensitive and helpful to others.

Let me do nothing today that will hurt anyone,
But let me help at least a little
To make life more pleasant for those I hurt.
When night comes, may I look back on this day
    without regrets
And may nobody be unhappy because of anything
I have done or failed to do.
Lord, bless this day for all of us.

Amen.

28 | Morning prayer

Every day I need thee, Lord,
but this day especially.
I need some extra strength
to face whatever is to be –
this day more than any day
I need to feel thee near
to fortify my courage
and overcome my fear.
By myself I cannot meet
the challenge of the hour,
there are times when human
creatures need a higher power
to help them bear what must be borne.
and so dear Lord I pray –
hold on to my trembling hand
and be with me today.

29 | Morning prayer

O God, early in the morning I cry to you.
Help me to pray
And to concentrate my thoughts on you.
I cannot do this alone.
In me there is darkness,
But with you there is light;
I am lonely, but you do not leave me;
I am feeble in heart, but with you there is help;
I am restless, but with you there is peace.
In me there is bitterness, but with you there is
     patience;
I do not understand your ways,
But you know the way for me ...
Restore me to liberty,

And enable me to live now
That I may answer before you and me.
Lord, whatever this day may bring,
Your name be praised.

Dietrich Bonhoeffer 1906 - 1945
written while awaiting execution in a Nazi prison

30 | Mothers

A mother is...

Someone who cares
    When others care less.
Someone who encourages
    When others ridicule.
Someone who defends
    When others condemn.
Someone with patience
    When others are impatient.
Someone who appreciates
    When others fail to notice.
Someone who gives security
    In a world of insecurity.
Someone who is accepting
    When others reject.
A mother is a friend for all time,
    To cherish and protect,
As her achievements will
    Linger for generations.

31 Mystical experience

Wherever a man's mind has been uplifted, his temptations thwarted, his sorrows comforted, his resolutions strengthened, his aberrations controlled by the sight of purity, innocence, love or beauty – indeed wherever he has, even for a moment, recognised and responded to the distinction between good and evil, between better and worse – such a man has had in part the mystical experience. Dim though his mirror may have been, he has yet seen God. Where he has seen God once there he may see him again... So far then from being rare, the mystical experience is at once the commonest and greatest of human accidents. There is not one of us to whom it does not come daily. It is only carelessness or custom that prevents our realising how divine it is in essence; only timidity which checks us from proclaiming that we too at such moments have seen God, even as if in a glass darkly... What Christianity offers, with its fellowship and sacraments, its life of prayer and service, its preaching of the Incarnate Son of God, is the same vision in ever-increasing plenitude...

K.E. Kirk 1886 - 1954

August

1 Neighbour

I sought my soul, the soul I could not see.
I sought my God and God eluded me.
I sought my brother and found all three.

2 Night prayer

Lord,
Forgive me for all the wrong I have done this day.
Forgive me if I have been bad tempered
    or hard to live with.
Forgive me if I have hurt those I should love.
Forgive me if I have made life more difficult for
    anyone.
Forgive me for any word of praise or thanks which I
    did not speak.
Forgive me for any help which I might have given to
    someone in need and did not give.
For any regrets I might have about today.
Help me to forgive myself as you forgive me.

Lord, bless our sick, our lonely, our neighbours and
    friends
And grant eternal rest to our dead.
Bless those who love me, and those I find it hard to
    forgive.
Lord, make me know the shortness of my life
That I may gain wisdom of heart.
God our Father, I come to say thank you for your
    love today.
Thank you for my family, and all the friends you
    give to me.
Guard me in the dark of night and in the morning
    send your light. Amen

3 | Nurse's prayer

Lord, give me grace on this and every day,
To do my work the best, not the simplest way;
And to remember that in all I do,
The very smallest task is seen by you.

Grant to me courage, Lord, when things go wrong,
To stop and think and not rush blindly on.
And though the task I'm set may not seem fair,
May I remember that thou too, art there.

Give me a humble heart that I may know,
That things worthwhile are not just things that show.
For though efficiency and skill mean much,
The greatest gift of all is human touch.

Fill me with love that I may realize
The suffering and pain that round me lies.
And grant each day that I may seek to share
The burdens of the people in my care.

Lord, give me strength to help me play my part,
To make my work the essence of my heart;
And show me patience and true kindness, Lord,
That I may spread thy radiance through my ward.

So when at night I come back to rest,
I pray that I may feel I've done my best.
And, Lord, at times I know I forget thee,
But please forgive, and always be with me. Amen.

Alwyn M. Law
published in New England *magazine*

4 | Old age

17th century nun's prayer

Lord, thou knowest better than I know myself that I am growing older, and will some day be old.

Keep me from getting talkative and particularly from the fatal habit of thinking I must say something on every subject and on every occasion.

Release me from craving to try to straighten out everybody's affairs.

Keep my mind free from the recital of endless details – give me wings to get to the point.

I ask for grace enough to listen to the tales of others' pains. Help me to endure them with patience.

But seal my lips on my own aches and pains – they are increasing, and my love of rehearsing them becomes sweeter as the years go by. Teach me the glorious lesson that occasionally it is possible that I may be mistaken. Keep me reasonably sweet; I do not want to be a saint – some of them are so hard to live with – but a sour old woman is one of the crowning works of the devil.

Make me thoughtful, but not moody; helpful but not bossy. With my vast store of wisdom it seems a pity not to use it all, but thou knowest, Lord, that I want a few friends at the end.

5 | Old age

To know how to grow old is the master work of wisdom, and one of the most difficult chapters in the great art of living.

Henri-Frédéric Amiel 1828 - 1881

6 | Old age

In old age

Father, help me to accept the lessening of my powers with realism and good humour.

Keep me from self pity and remind me that age has not taken my mission in life – only altered it.

Grant me a taste for the hidden beauties of creation, a continuing interest in your world – and mine.

Make me more patient with myself, more tolerant with the failures of others, more outgoing with the timid and shy.

Bestow on me a greater readiness for prayer, and a humble acceptance of suffering.

Deepen my faith in your unfailing truth. Strengthen my hope that I will share in your Son's resurrection.

Expand my love in your Holy Spirit for all men, with whom I am destined to share in the fellowship of the blessed for all eternity. Amen.

7 | Old age

Old age is something to be worn with dignity, knowing that you've lived and seen and experienced so many things that can be useful to the young.

Josephine Baker

8 Opportunities

There is a tide in the affairs of men
Which taken at the flood leads on to fortune;
Omitted, all the voyage of their life
Is bound in shallows and in miseries.
On such a full sea are we now afloat,
And we must take the current when it serves,
Or lose our ventures.

William Shakespeare 1564 - 1616

9 Optimism

The optimist Creed

To be so strong that nothing can disturb your peace of mind.

To talk health, happiness and prosperity to every person you meet.

To make all your friends feel that there is something in them.

To look at the sunny side of everything and make your optimism come true.

To think only of the best, to work only for the best, and to expect only the best.

To be just as enthusiastic about the success of others as you are about your own.

To forget the mistakes of the past and press on to the greater achievements of the future.

To wear a cheerful countenance at all times and give every living creature you meet a smile.

To give so much time to the improvement of yourself that you have no time to criticise others.

To be too large for worry, too noble for anger, too strong for fear, and too happy to permit the presence of trouble.

10 Oratory

Nothing serves an orator better than profound conviction.

St Vincent de Paul c. 1580 - 1660

11 Others

Lord, help me to live from day to day
In such a self forgetful way,
That even when I kneel to pray,
My prayers shall be for
"OTHERS"

Help me in all the work I do
Ever to be sincere and true,
And know that all I do for you
Must needs be done for
"OTHERS"

Let self be crucified and slain
And buried deep and all in vain
Its efforts be to rise again
Unless to live for
"OTHERS"

And when my work on earth is done
And my new work in heaven's begun
May I forget the crown I've won,
While thinking still for
"OTHERS"

"OTHERS," Lord, yes, "OTHERS"
Let this my motto be.
Help me to live for "OTHERS"
For then I live for thee.

contributed by Cardinal Jaime L. Sin

12 Others

Hear me, Lord, on behalf of all those who are dear
   to me,
All whom I have in mind at this moment.
Be near them in all their anxieties and worries.
Give them the help of thy saving grace.
I commend them all with trustful confidence to thy
   merciful love.

Remember, Lord, all who are mindful of me;
All who have asked me to pray for them;
All who have been kind to me;
All who have wronged me, or whom I have
   wronged by ill will or misunderstanding.

Give all of us grace to bear each others faults,
And to share each other's burdens.
Have mercy on the souls of our loved ones who
   have gone before us.
Grant them peace and happiness. Amen.

Canon Gordon Albion 1906 - 1979

13 Parents

Overlook nothing, absolutely nothing, that could
contribute to the good moral and intellectual development of your children, nor anything that might be of
value in your own interior spiritual progress. There
must be no economising on good books. If souls
consecrated to God, monks who think about perfection
from morning to night, feel the need right to the end of
their lives to read and reread the works of the masters
of the spiritual life and the lives of the saints who have
gone before them, how much more must they need it

who live in the world, in the middle of so many distract-
ing occupations?... Trust, trust, be free of all anxiety.
Bring up your children well for God's sake and God
will arrange their future a hundred thousand times better
than you, or all the people in the world put together,
could do.

Charles de Foucauld 1858 - 1916

14 Patience

When little things would irk me and I grow
Impatient with my dear ones, make me know
How in a moment joy can take its flight
And happiness be quenched in endless night.
Keep this thought with me all the livelong day,
That I may guard the harsh words I might say,
When I would fret and grumble fiery hot,
At trifles that tomorrow are forgot.
Let me remember, Lord, how it would be
If these, my loved ones, were not here with me.

15 Pattern for living

1. Make up your mind to be happy. Learn to find
   pleasure in simple things.

2. Make the best of your circumstances. No one has
   everything and everyone has something of sorrow
   intermingled with the gladness of life. The trick is
   to make the laughter outweigh the tears.

3. Don't take yourself too seriously. Don't think that
   somehow you should be protected from misfor-
   tunes that befall others.

4. You can't please everybody. Don't let criticism hurt you.

5. Don't let your neighbours set your standards. Be yourself.

6. Do the things you enjoy doing, but stay out of debt.

7. Don't borrow trouble. Imaginary things are harder to bear than the actual ones.

8. Since hate poisons the soul, do not cherish enmities, grudges. Avoid people who make you unhappy.

9. Have many interests. If you can't travel, read about new places.

10. Don't hold post-mortems. Don't spend your life brooding over sorrows or mistakes. Don't be one who never gets over things.

11. Do what you can for those less fortunate than yourself.

12. Keep busy at something. A busy person never has time to be unhappy.

Robert Louis Stephenson 1850 - 1894

16 Peace

Lord, make me an instrument of your peace.
    Where there is hatred, let me show love,
    Where there is injury, pardon;
    Where there is doubt, faith;
    Where there is despair, hope;
    Where there is darkness, light;
    Where there is sadness, joy.

O Divine Master,
Grant that I may not so much seek
    To be consoled, as to console,
    To be understood, as to understand,
    To be loved, as to love,
    For it is in giving that we receive;
    It is in pardoning that we are pardoned;
    It is in dying that we are born to eternal life.

St Francis of Assisi 1181 - 1226

17 Peace

Loving Father,
perfect teacher,
patient guide
in these troubled times;
sitting with you,
the perfect One,
I take the influence
of your company
to teach me
the way of reconciliation,
wisdom and harmony.
I see you,
the embodiment of all solutions
for the world
and myself at this time.
Touch my heart
and my conscience daily,
that all I do
will work towards
your goal of perfection
and peace for mankind.

18 Peace

O Spirit of God,
Set at rest the crowded, hurrying, conscious
thoughts within our minds and hearts.
Let the peace and quiet of your presence take possession of us.
Help us to relax, to rest, to become open and receptive to you.
You know our inmost spirit, the hidden unconscious
life within us, the forgotten memories of hurts and
fears, the frustrated desires, the unresolved tensions
and dilemmas.
Cleanse and sweeten the springs of our being
that freedom, life and love may flow into both our
conscious and hidden life.
Lord, we lie open before you, waiting for your healing, your peace and your word.

George Appleton

19 People

Do not despise others because, as it seems to you, they
do not possess the virtues you thought they had; they
may be pleasing to God for other reasons which you
cannot discover.

St John of the Cross 1542 - 1591

20 Perseverance

Go bravely on doing the daily duties and trusting that
as our day is, so shall our strength be.

Edward King 1829 - 1910

21 Petition

Time after time I came to your gate
With raised hands, asking for more and yet more.
You gave and gave, now in slow measure, now in
    sudden excess,
I took some things and some things I let drop;
Some lay heavy on my hands; some I made into
    playthings
And broke them when tired; 'till the wrecks of the
    hoard
Of your gifts grew immense, hiding you.
The ceaseless expectation wore my heart out.

Take, O take – has now become my cry.
Shatter all from this beggar's bowl:
Put out this lamp of the importunate watcher:
Hold my hands, raise me from the still-gathering
    heap of your gifts
Into the bare infinity of your uncrowded presence.

Rabindranath Tagore 1861 - 1941

22 Potential

Did you know you're a wonderful person?
Full of love and countless good deeds.
Your unselfishness is a lesson
That most of humanity needs.
In humbleness you're a great leader.
Status and earthly trappings
You scorn as illusory things;
You're the same in whatever company,
Be it a tramp or a king;
You hold in your hand the light
Of love and honesty.

This is your own potential,
All this inner beauty I see.
You're just an ordinary person
With the choice of what you can be.
The start to change is so simple,
We become what we think and believe,
So don't waste your life in the darkness,
It's not human life's destiny;
And apart from life's materialism
There's nothing we cannot achieve.
Did you know, deep down within you,
There is a wonderful person
Full of love and countless deeds.

David Brown

23 | Poverty

The poor and the weak have revealed to me
the great secret of Jesus.
If you wish to follow him
you must not try to climb the ladder of
success and power,
becoming more and more important.
Instead, you must walk *down* the ladder,
to meet and walk with people
who are broken and in pain.
The light is there, shining in the darkness,
in the darkness of their poverty.
The poor with whom you are called to share your
life
and perhaps the sick and the old;
people out of work
young people caught up in the world of drugs,
people angry because they were terribly hurt
when they were young,

people with disabilities or sick with AIDS,
or just out of prison;
people in slums or ghettos,
people in far-off lands
where there is much hunger and suffering,
people who are oppressed
because of the colour of their skin,
people who are lonely in overcrowded cities,
people in pain.

Jean Vanier

24 Poverty

Indeed, no other devotion of the faithful is more pleasing to the Lord than that which is directed towards his poor.

Where he finds merciful concern he recognises the reflection of his own kindness.

Pope St Leo the Great d. 461

25 Poverty

The poor are the hungry and the thirsty.
The poor are those who go about in rags.
The poor are the homeless.
The poor are the sick.

The poor are the physically and mentally
    handicapped.
The poor are the old.
The poor are the imprisoned.
The poor are the sad and depressed.

135

The poor are those who suffer injustice.
The poor are the unemployed and those on low
 wages.
The poor are the rejects and unwanted.
The poor are the lonely and the unloved.

The poor, in one way or another, are we ourselves.
Before God we are all poor.
May we never see poverty as a curse from God.
Rather may we know that when we are poor
the Kingdom of heaven is ours.

Flor McCarthy SDB

26 Poverty

The poor we see with the eyes of the flesh. They are
present. We can put our fingers and our hands into
their wounds. The marks of the crown of thorns are
plainly visible on their heads. We should fall at their
feet and say to them: "You are our masters, we should
be your servants; you are the visible image of the God
whom we do not see, but whom we love in loving you."

Frédéric Ozanam 1813 - 1853

27 Prayer

I said a prayer for you today,
And know God must have heard –
I felt the answer in my heart
Although he spoke no word!
I didn't ask for wealth or fame
(I knew you wouldn't mind) –
I asked him to send treasures
Of a far more lasting kind!

I asked that he be near you
At the start of each new day
To grant you health and blessings
And friends to share your way.
I asked for happiness for you
In all things great and small –
But it was for his loving care
I prayed the most of all!
God be with you

28 | Prayer

The ultimate way to God, in all traditions, is through silence, through the hidden martyrdom of prayer. When all words, all thoughts, all feelings, all images are set aside and we rest in the darkness, like a seed in the earth, then he reveals himself to us and we learn our true identity, for he is both the journey and the journey's end.

James Roose-Evans

29 | Prayer

When a man closes his lips, God begins to speak.

Hazrat Inayat Khan

30 | Prayer

If you make a habit of sincere prayer, your life will be very noticeably and profoundly altered. Prayer stamps with its indelible mark our actions and demeanour. A

tranquillity of bearing, a facial and bodily repose, are
observed in those whose inner lives are thus enriched.

Alexis Carrel

31 Prayer (in times of illness)

Take my hand

I cannot pray, dear Lord. I cannot find
The hopes; recovery; health; and peace of mind.

And yet, although you suffered more than I
This does not help, no matter how I try.

So, take my hand, and take my feeble frame
And give me strength, and help me bear my pain.

And though my future plans may go astray
In all my fears be near. Show me the way.

I am so weak – give me the strength I need
To know that with Your help, we will succeed.

So, help me in these long and tiring days
To know that someone sings a song of praise.

The friends who care, who pray instead of me,
For healing and a quick recovery.

So, take my hand, and let me cling to thee
And clinging – know no harm can come to me.

C.M. Ford

September

1 Prayer

There must be some of you tonight
who feel you'll never smile again,
who reel beneath the cruel blow
of sudden tragedy or pain.
It may seem quite beyond your power
to face alone your empty plight.
Well, make no quick decisions now.
Just kneel and say your prayers tonight.

Jean Morton

2 Prayer

The power of prayer

The day was long, the burden I had borne
Seemed heavier than I could longer bear,
And then it lifted – but I did not know
Someone had knelt in prayer;
Had taken me to God that very hour,
And asked the easing of the load, and he,
In infinite compassion, had stooped down
And taken it from me.
We cannot tell how often as we pray
For some bewildered one, hurt and distressed,
The answer comes, but many times those hearts
Find sudden peace and rest.
Someone had prayed, and faith, a reaching hand,
Took hold of God, and brought him down that day!
So many, many hearts have need of prayer:
Oh, let us pray!

3 | Prayer

A person who is too busy to pray is too busy.

•••

Prayer is the key that opens the morning
and the safety bolt at the end of the day.

•••

Seven prayer-less days makes one weak.

•••

Prayer does not change God
but it changes him who prays.

4 | Prayer

Don't imagine that if you had a great deal of time you
would spend more of it in prayer. Get rid of that idea!
Again and again God gives more in a moment than in
a longer period of time, for his actions are not meas-
ured by time at all.

St Teresa of Avila 1515 - 1582

5 | Prayer

Great talent is a gift of God, but it is a gift which is by
no means necessary in order to pray well. This gift is
required in order to converse well with men; but it is
not necessary in order to speak well with God. For that,
one needs good desires, and nothing more.

St John of the Cross 1542 - 1591

6 Prayer

If you do not pray, everything can disappoint you by going wrong.

If you do pray, everything can still go wrong, but not in a way that will disappoint you.

Hubert Van Zeller OSB

7 Prayer

Lift up your heart to him sometimes even at your meals and when you are in company; the least little remembrance will always be acceptable to him. You need not cry very loud; he is nearer to us than we are aware of. We may make an oratory of our heart wherein to retire from time to time, to converse with him in meekness, humility and love.

Brother Lawrence 1624 - 1691

8 Prayer

God, I thank you for this time of prayer, when I become conscious of your presence, and lay before you my desires, my hopes, and my gratitude. This consciousness, this inner certainty of your presence is my greatest blessing. My life would be empty if I did not have it, if I lost you in the maze of the world, and I did not return to you from time to time, to be at one with you, certain of your existence and your love. It is good that you are with me in all my difficulties and troubles and that I have in you a friend whose help is sure and whose love never changes.

from Forms of Prayer for Jewish Worship

9 | Prayer

Prayer is nothing more than the interior life in action, the whole man giving God his undivided attention. Not to pray means not to be aware of the presence of God. Further, it signifies that a man is not present to himself at the basic levels of his own being. Far from constituting an alienating element, prayer is rather the element that cements man and gives him unity.

J.M. Cabodevilla

10 | Prayer

In the peace of solitude
I close my eyes in order to see
For I know that in the silence
You will come to me.
From my heart I speak
The words of thanks and praise,
Even the unspoken word
I know will reach you as I pray.
I call upon your Spirit, Lord,
To guide me in my prayer;
The door gently opens
I see you standing there.
I see you in my mind's eye
I feel you all around
As we commune, you and I
Yet making not a sound.
When I cannot find the words
To tell you of my love
My spirit speaks its own tongue
Flying on the wings of a dove.
My spirit and yours
As one in unison
I burn within your fire

142

The flames growing; on and on
Until the world becomes a memory.
You, Lord, are the reality.
Oh how beautiful this time,
Just one moment in eternity.

Carol Wood

11 Prayer

Why has our sincere prayer for each other such great power over others? Because of the fact that by cleaving to God during prayer I become one spirit with him, and unite with myself, by faith and love, those for whom I pray; for the Holy Spirit acting in me also acts at the same time in them, for he accomplishes all things.

John of Cronstadt 1829 - 1908

12 Prayer

I thank thee, Lord, for knowing me better than I know myself, and for letting me know myself better than others know me.

Make me, I pray thee, better than they suppose, and forgive me for what they do not know.

Abu Bekr ?572 - 634

13 Prayer

Accustom yourself gradually to carry prayer into all your daily occupations. Speak, move, work, in peace, as if you were in prayer, as indeed you ought to be. Do

everything without excitement, by the spirit of grace.
As soon as you perceive your natural impetuosity glid-
ing in, retire quietly within, where is the kingdom of
God. Listen to the leadings of grace, then say and do
nothing but what the Holy Spirit shall put in your heart.
You will find that you will become more tranquil, that
your words will be fewer and more effectual, and that,
with less effort, you will accomplish more good.

François Fénélon 1651 - 1715

14 Prayer

Oft have I seen at some cathedral door
A labourer, pausing in the dust and heat,
Lay down his burden, and with reverent feet
Enter and cross himself his paternoster o'er;
Far off the noises of the world retreat;
The loud vociferations of the street
Become an indistinguishable roar.

So, as I enter here from day to day,
And leave my burden at this minster gate,
Kneeling in prayer, and not ashamed to pray,
The tumult of the time disconsolate
To inarticulate murmurs dies away,
While the eternal ages watch and wait.

Henry Wadsworth Longfellow 1807 - 1882

15 Prayer

My prayer to God is a very short one:

"O Lord make my enemies most ridiculous!"

God has granted it.

Voltaire 1694 - 1778

16 Prayer

He didn't actually accuse God of inefficiency, but when he prayed his tone was loud and angry, like that of a dissatisfied guest in a carelessly managed hotel!

Clarence Day

17 Prayer

The justification for spending time and energy in praying is similar to the justification the mountaineer gave for wanting to climb Everest – "Because it is there!" God is there. So we pray. We circle him in adoration and surrender ourselves back to him. It is true that we can walk with God and speak to him all day as we go about our daily work surrendering to him in the midst of his creation and giving him everything we do from moment to moment. But thank God we can do more; and it is this doing more which makes Christianity exciting. We can give God more than our daily work. We can give him ourselves. We can give him our time. We can go deep in prayer.

John Dalrymple 1928 - 1985

18 Prayer

Prayer is turning the mind and thoughts toward God. To pray means to stand before God with the mind, mentally to gaze unswervingly at him, and to converse with him in reverent fear and hope.

St Dimitri of Rostov

19 Preaching

That the preaching of these men was indeed divine is clearly brought home to us when we consider how else could twelve uneducated men, who lived on lakes and rivers and wastelands, get the idea for such an immense enterprise? How could men who perhaps had never been in a city or a public forum think of setting out to do battle with the whole world?

St John Chrysostom c. 347 - 407

20 Priesthood

If the priest preaches more than ten minutes, he is
    too long-winded,
If his sermon is short, he is too easy-going.
If the parish funds are low, he's a bad businessman,
If he mentions money, he's too grasping.
If he visits his parishioners, he's never home,
If he doesn't, he's snobbish.
If he runs bazaars and ballots, he's bleeding the
    people
If he doesn't, the parish is lacking social life.
If he takes time in the confessional, he's too slow,
If he doesn't, he has no time for people.

If he starts Mass on the minute, his watch is fast,
If he's a bit late, he's holding up the congregation.
If he decorates the church, he's spending too much,
If he doesn't, he's letting it run down.
If he's young, he's inexperienced,
If he's old, he should retire.

If he dies, there will never be his equal again!

21 | Priesthood

My dear friends, accept us as we are:
the priest is not an angel sent from heaven.
He is a man, chosen from among men,
a member of the Church, a Christian.
Remaining man and Christian, he begins to
speak to you the Word of God. This Word
is not his own; he speaks it because God
has told him to proclaim his Word. Perhaps
he has not entirely understood it himself,
perhaps he adulterates it, but he believes,
and despite his fears, he knows that he must
communicate God's Word to you. For must not
some one of us say something about God, about
eternal life, about the majesty of grace in
our sanctified being; must not someone of us
speak of sin and of the judgement and mercy
of God? So, my dear friends, pray for us,
carry us, so that we might be able to sustain
others by bringing to them the mystery of God's
love revealed in Christ Jesus our Lord.

Karl Rahner SJ 1904 - 1984

22 Priorities

Remember that you have only one soul;
that you have only one death to die;
that you have only one life, which is
short and has to be lived by you alone;
and there is only one glory, which is eternal.
If you do this, there will be many things
about which you care nothing.

St Teresa of Avila 1515 - 1582

23 Purpose

Be this the central faith and fact of life; that there is a
light beyond our darkness, and a purpose which makes
music of our confusion – and we, you and I, have some
part in both. Hold fast to that and fear nothing.

Gerald Buffett

24 Purpose

Never worry about being useful. When you have become
God's in the measure he wants, he himself will know
how to bestow you on others.

Anon.

25 Quietness

I needed the quiet so he drew me aside,
into the shadows where we could confide;
away from the hustle where all the day long

I hurried and worried when active and strong.
I needed the quiet though at first I rebelled,
but gently, so gently, my cross he upheld,
and whispered so sweetly of spiritual things,
though weakened in body my spirit took wings
to heights never dreamed of when active and strong.
He loved me so gently he drew me along.
I needed the quiet, no prison my bed
but a beautiful valley of blessing instead;
a place to grow richer, in Jesus to hide,
I needed the quiet so he drew me aside.

Cardinal Richard Cushing 1895 - 1970

26 Reconciliation

Remember that the confessor is a father who is eager
to do all he can for you and protect you from all possible
harm. Never fear that you will lose his respect when
confessing serious sins, or that he will reveal them to
others. No matter what may happen to him, the confessor may never avail himself of any information received
in the confessional. Should he stand to lose his life, he
can not and will not tell anyone at all even the slightest
thing heard in confessional. Moreover, I can assure you
that the more sincere and trusting you are with him, the
more his confidence in you will grow and the better he
will be able to give you that advice and counsel which
he deems most necessary and useful for your soul.

St John Bosco 1815 - 1888

27 Reconciliation – a litany

Almighty God, creator of life, sustainer of every good thing I know, my partner with me in the pain of this earth, hear my prayer as I am in the midst of separation and alienation from everything I know to be supportive, and healing, and true...

AIDS has caused me to feel separated from you. I say, "Why me, what did I do to deserve this?"... Help me to remember that you do not punish your creation by bringing disease, but that you are Emmanuel, God with us. You are as close to me as my next breath.

AIDS has caused a separation between the body I knew and my body now... Help me to remember that I am more than my body and, while it pains me greatly to see what has happened to it, I am more than my body... I am part of you and you me.

AIDS has separated me from my family... Oh God help me and them to realise that I haven't changed, I'm still their child, our love for each other is your love for us... Help them overcome their fear, embarrassment and guilt... Their love brought me into this world... Help them share as much as possible with me.

AIDS has caused a separation between me and my friends; my friendships have been so important to me. They are especially important now... Help me oh God to recognise their fear, and help them to realise my increasing need for them to love in any way they can.

AIDS has separated me from my society, my work world and my community... It pains me for them to see me differently now... Forgive them for allowing their ignorance of this disease and their fear to blind their judgements... Help me with my anger towards them.

AIDS has caused a separation between me and my Church... Help the Church restore its ministry to 'the least of these' by reaching out to me and others... Help them suspend their judgements and love me as they have before... Help me and them to realise that the Church is the Body of Christ... that separation and alienation wound the body.

God of my birth and God of my death, help me know you have been, you are, and you are to come... Amen.

Written by an unknown author living with AIDS

28 | Religion

Among all my patients in the second half of life – that is to say, over thirty-five – there has not been one whose problem in the last resort was not that of finding a religious outlook on life. It is safe to say that every one of them fell ill because he had lost that which the living religions of every age have given to their followers, and none of them has been really healed who did not regain his religious outlook.

Carl G. Jung 1875 - 1961

29 | Religious experience

Religious experience at its roots is experience of an unconditional and unrestricted being in love. But what we are in love with remains something that we have to find out.

Bernard Lonergan SJ 1904 - 1984

30 | Remembrance

For the fallen

They shall not grow old,
as we that are left grow old:
Age shall not weary them,
nor the years condemn.
At the going down of the sun
and in the morning
We will remember them.

Laurence Binyon 1869 - 1943

October

1 | Resilience

Resiliency is an important factor in living. The winds of life may bend us, but if we have resilience of spirit, they cannot break us. To courageously straighten again after our heads have been bowed by defeat, disappointment and suffering, is the supreme test of character.

Anon.

2 | Risk taking

To laugh is to risk appearing the fool.
To weep is to risk appearing sentimental.
To reach out for another is to risk involvement.
To expose feeling is to risk exposing your true self.
To place your ideas, your dreams before the crowd
    is to risk their loss.
To love is to risk not being loved in return.
To live is to risk dying.
To hope is to risk despair.
To try is to risk failure.

But the risk must be taken, because
    the greater hazard in life is to risk nothing.
The person who risks nothing,
    does nothing, has nothing, and is nothing.
He may avoid suffering and sorrow,
    but he simply cannot learn, feel, change, grow,
    love, live.
Chained by his certitudes, he is a slave;
    he has forfeited freedom.

Only a person who risks is free!

3 | Sabbath

Lord of all creation, you have made us the masters of your world, to tend it, to serve it, and to enjoy it. For six days we measure and we build, we count and carry the real and the imagined burdens of our task, the success we earn and the price we pay.

On this, the Sabbath day, give us rest.

For six days if we are weary or bruised by the world, if we think ourselves giants or cause others pain, there is never a moment to pause, and know what we should really be.

On this, the Sabbath day, give us rest.

For six days we are torn between our private greed and the urgent needs of others, between the foolish noises in our ears and the silent prayer of our soul.

On this, the Sabbath day, give us rest.

Help us, Lord, to carry these lessons, of rest and time, of understanding and peace, into the six days that lie ahead, to bless us in the working days of our lives. Amen.

Jewish prayer for the Sabbath

4 | Sacrament of the sick

There are other times when we think of death, and more particularly of our own. It is common destiny and has to be reckoned with. It helps us to get the measure of life and what is important, and we have to see it in God's plan as a decisive moment when we shall be judged. Apart from sudden deaths there comes a time when we become more acutely conscious of the possibility and prospect of our own death. It can come through grave illness, or the advancing frailty of old age, or a serious accident. We may not be actually dying, but death is a more real prospect. In the Church we celebrate a sacrament for this time in our life. It is more commonly known now as the Anointing of the sick. We come together with the priest to open up our weak condition, our frail mortality, to the presence of Christ and welcome him as the Saviour, the healer of our ills, one who can change our sinfulness and our feebleness into a situation of faith that still has about it the strong promise of life, the life that he came to bring which will endure into everlasting life. This is a great sacrament that restores hope at a time when we are losing strength, hope perhaps of recovery, but hope above all in God the giver of life whose Son has redeemed us.

Do not neglect this sacrament. I have received it five times this year as illness struck me or entered upon a new phase. There was a time when some people saw it as a sentence of death, whereas it is full of the promise of life. It is Christ coming to reassure us that he is still at our side in our journey of faith and when the going seems to get harder.

Bishop Francis Thomas 1930 - 1988

5 | Saints

The saints give little thought to changing the world around them. They are too busy changing the world within them. They are not out to reform Caesar, but to conform themselves to Christ. They were reconcilers not revolutionists. Ideas have consequences. The divine ideas that filled the mind of the saints have had, and continue to have, sublime consequences in history.

Clare Boothe Luce

6 Saints

It was because the saints were absorbed in God that they were truly capable of seeing and appreciating created things, and it was because they loved him alone that they alone loved everybody.

Thomas Merton 1915 - 1968

7 Searching

With the drawing of this Love and the voice of this
    Calling
We shall not cease from exploration,
And the end of all our exploring
Will be to arrive where we started
And know the place for the first time.

T.S. Eliot 1888 - 1965

8 Searching

Too late have I known you,
O everlasting truth.
Too late have I loved you,
O beauty always old and ever new.

Behold! You were within
And I looked for you elsewhere
And in my weakness I ran after the beauty
in the things you have made.

You were in me and I was not with you.
The things you created kept me far from you.
You have called. You have cried out,
and have pierced my deafness.
You have shone forth,
and have lifted my blindness.
You have sent forth your sweetness
and I have longed after you
and looked for you.
I have tasted you.
And now my whole hope is in nothing else
but in your very great mercy,
O Lord, my God.

For he does not really love you,
who loves anything else,
which he does not love for your sake.

O Love which always burns and never grows less,
true charity, my God, set me all on fire.
Give me what you command,
and command what you wish.

All-powerful God,
you care for each one of us
as if you loved him alone,
and you care for all,
as if all were but one.

Things of this world pass away
that others may replace them,
but you never pass away
or never depart.

O God our Father supremely good,
Beauty of all things beautiful,
to you we entrust
whatsoever we have received from you.
Through Jesus Christ our Lord. Amen.

St Augustine 354 - 430

9 | Seasons

The changing seasons

These then are the changing seasons and how like
to man they are, from birth to youth, full blooded
manhood and old age, to disappear white faced
beneath our mother earth and like all things to
reappear in glorious risen spirit.
Not for man the decay of mortality and oblivion,
but an eternity in everlasting creation,
loved for all time, by an unchanging, never ending
God, who was, who is and always will be, the
wondrous hand that
wrought the magic of the universe and our world,
whose love knows no bounds, whose wisdom
and knowledge lies still unfathomed in the infinite vastness of the future, where lies all man's
hopes and expectations.
Look then upon the changing seasons with all their
mysterious magic as a small act of God's love for
man, and though we cannot return it measure for
measure – return it love for love.

10 | Self

Self-inventory for these new beginning days

I believe in me – my worth as a human being, created
and loved by God. I am unique. There is only one of
me.

Intellectually I have my abilities. I can open my mind
to new ideas. I can make decisions. I can read and
absorb what I read. I can judge, think and act.

I have inward strength. I can face life and I can face death. I refused to give up before when the going was rough. I can keep on going now.

I care about other people. I can love. I can show concern outside myself. I can entertain other people for a meal or share a cup of coffee. I can be a friend. I can reach out to others. I can love my family and be loved by them in return.

I can believe enough in myself that "what other people think" need not frighten me. I can be me without fear. I do not need to meet the standards set for me by other people. I am capable of setting standards for myself, of honesty, of social living, of personal life.

I believe in my ideals, symbolised in the cross I wear. I can accept myself as lovable by others, for who and what I am.

I AM GOD'S CHILD! I believe in me.

Lois Mae Cubel

11 Serenity prayer

God grant me the SERENITY
to accept the things
I cannot change...
COURAGE to change
the things I can
and WISDOM to
know the difference.

12 | Service

The moment we understand that we are no more than instruments of God is a beautiful one.

Archbishop Oscar Romero 1917 - 1980

13 | Sick, The

Cheer up, God is with you. You suffer, it is true. But he is near you, trust in him as you would your own father. If he has let you suffer, it is because he sees something in it which today you do not yet know. Your peace of mind is in your trust in God who can never let you down.

Pope John Paul II

14 | Sickness, In

A cry for help

My life is one long struggle, Lord,
  And you can help me bear it.
I know I can get through each day
  With you beside to share it.

Please take my hurting body, Lord,
  And ease my every pain.
Just hold me in your loving arms
  Until I'm well again.

You knew what weakness was, dear Lord,
  Give me the strength I need.
Your everlasting arms beneath
  To help me to succeed.

160

Stay close beside me every hour
    And hear me when I call.
I need thee, how I need thee, Lord
    My love – my life – my all.

C.M. Ford

15 | Silence

We need to find God and he cannot be found in noise
and restlessness. God is the friend of silence. See how
nature – trees, flowers, grass – grow in silence; see the
stars, the moon, the sun, how they move in silence. Is
not our mission to give God to the poor in the slums?
Not a dead God, but a living, loving God. The more we
receive in silent prayer, the more we can give in our
active life. We need silence to be able to touch souls.
The essential thing is not what we say, but what God
says to us and through us. All our words will be useless
unless they come from within – words which do not
give the light of Christ increase the darkness.

Mother Teresa of Calcutta

16 | Silence

I am in love with Love

I am in love with Love,
And Love is God.
I am in love with the Silence
Where he dwells;
With the solitude where he walks;
I rest in a pool of peace,

And I am still in the stillness, where he
Stands transfigured, and in that stillness I
Rest in love at his feet.

Winifred M. Eddison

17 | Silence

    Strange vagabond that knows not what to seek
The rest you lack lies not this far afield.
    Much babel tumult makes your hearing weak
And all replete with sights your eyes are sealed.
    Far out you have strayed to find your inmost soul
But souls their eloquence in stillness find.
    Be still then, let God's silence make you whole
For he alone can calm your troubled mind.
    Your heart's desire is nearest though unseen
Your haven of perfection close at hand
    And that drear quest was as a fevered dream
God's love within you is your native land.
    So search none other, never more depart
For you are homeless, save God keeps your heart.

John Dove SJ

18 | Silence

When the heart is hard and parched up,
come upon me with a shower of mercy.

When grace is lost from life,
come with a burst of song.

When the tumultuous work raises its din
on all sides shutting me out from beyond,
come to me,
my lord of silence,
with thy peace and rest.

Rabindranath Tagore 1861-1941

19 | Silence

Silence and the enclosure provide the time and space
to open ourselves to a greater invasion of God's love.

A contemplative nun

20 | Silence

Oh, in the time of silence when man remains alone,
abandoned when he does not hear thy voice, it seems
to him doubtless that the separation must last forever.
Oh, in the time of silence when a man consumes himself
in the desert in which he does not hear thy voice, it
seems to him doubtless that it is completely extinguished.
Father in heaven! It is only a moment of silence in an
intimacy of conversation. Bless then this silence as thy
word to man; grant he never forgets that thou speakest
also when thou art silent; give him this consolation if
he waits on thee, that thou art silent through love, that
thou speakest through love, so that in thy silence as in
thy word thou art still the same Father and that it is still
the same paternal love that thou guidest by thy voice
and that thou dost instruct by thy silence.

Sören Kierkegaard 1813 - 1855

21 Silence

I listen to the silence,
For then memories have their sway:
Memories buried in the past,
Too weak to penetrate the day.
But in the silence
I hear them sharp and clear:
Memories of strife,
Struggle and fear,
Creating grief
Without relief.
Yet, in the silence
They are softened,
Muted with age,
And the silence tells me
Each memory was a page
Printed for my life,
A page I had to read,
Then act, to complete the play
That has brought me
To the chapter
In which I comprehend
That in silence was the beginning,
And in silence is the end.

Catherine Cookson

22 Sin

The Lord will never ask how successful we were in overcoming a particular sin or imperfection. he will ask: "Did you humbly and patiently bear this mystery of iniquity in your life? How did you deal with it? Did it teach you not to trust in your own ability but in my love? Did it enable you to understand and be compassionate with the mystery of iniquity in the lives of others?

164

Did it above all give you the most typical characteristic of the truly religious person – that he never judges or condemns the sin of others? The Christian knows from his own life that the demon of evil can be stronger than man ... he knows that it is the patience, charity and humility learned which counts. Success or failure are accidental. The joy of the Christian is never based on his personal religious success, but on the knowledge that his Redeemer lives.

Adrian van Kamm

23 | Sinners

Of course the fear that one's infidelity is being punished is just a stupid temptation. Our Lord came to save *sinners*, and we must not frustrate him by saying, "*Because* I have been a sinner, therefore I'm shut out from his mercy". The devil would love us to say that but then he is the father of lies.

Bishop Christopher Butler OSB 1902 - 1986

24 | Sinners

When Christ wished to teach us what God is like he pointed to the God-like in men. Even in the worst sinner he could discover the hidden good and appeal to it, knowing that the good and not the evil is the essential man. He tells us that it is when a sinner "comes to himself" that he "arises and goes to his Father": the man's true self is that within him which responds to God.

G.H.C. MacGregor

25 | Solitude

I discover more and more each day my need for these times of solitude in which I can rediscover others with more truth, and accept in the light of God my own weakness, ignorance, egoism and fear. This solitude does not separate me from others: it helps me love them more tenderly, realistically and attentively. I begin to distinguish between the false solitude which is a flight from others to be alone with egoism, sadness and a bruised sensitivity, and true solitude which is a communion with God and others.

Jean Vanier

26 | Solitude

It is God's work, God who encloses you in the tabernacle of his hiddeness, so that you and he may enjoy one another alone. There the lonely, the unwanted, the undesirable, can find one as lonely, as unwanted, as undesirable as themselves. This low estate is the precious link which unites the solitary soul to God, himself the great solitary.

Pere Gallore, 17th century

27 | Solitude

For the man or woman who has come to know and love the Lord God in the depths of such intimacy, the times of solitude are the most precious in all of life. They are a rendezvous with the beloved. They are anticipated with eagerness. They are awaited with expectancy... For the person who has found in God a truly loving heavenly Father, gentle interludes with him alone are highlights of life. For the one who has found Christ the

166

dearest friend among all the children of earth, quiet times in his company are the oases of life. For the individual, conscious of the comradeship of God's gracious Spirit in the stillness of solitude, these intervals are the elixir of life.

W. Phillip Keller

28 | Solitude

In solitude we discover that being is more important than having, and that we are worth more than the result of our efforts. In solitude we discover that our life is not a possession to be defended, but a gift to be shared. It's there we recognise that the healing words we speak are not just our own but are given to us: that the love we express is part of a greater love; and the new life we bring forth is not a property to cling to but a gift to be received.

Henri Nouwen

29 | Solitude

To go up alone into the mountain and come back as an ambassador to the world, has ever been the method of humanity's best friends.

Evelyn Underhill 1875 - 1941

30 | Sorrow

Can I see another's woe,
And not be in sorrow too?
Can I see another's grief,
And not seek for kind relief?

Can I see a falling tear,
And not feel my sorrow's share?
Can a father see his child
Weep, nor be with sorrow filled?

Can a mother sit and hear
An infant groan, an infant's fear?
No, no! never can it be!
Never, never can it be!

And can he who smiles on all
Hear the wren with sorrows small,
Hear the small bird's grief and care,
Hear the woes that infants bear –

And not sit beside the nest,
Pouring pity in their breast,
And not sit the cradle near,
Weeping tear on infant's tear?

And not sit both night and day,
Wiping all our tears away?
Oh no! never can it be!
Never, never can it be!

He doth give his joy to all:
He becomes an infant small,
He becomes a man of woe,
He doth feel the sorrow too.

Think not thou canst sigh a sigh,
And thy Maker is not by:
Think not thou canst weep a tear,
And thy Maker is not near.

Oh, he gives to us his joy,
That our grief he may destroy:
Till our grief is fled and gone
He doth sit by us and moan.

William Blake 1757 - 1827

31 | Special

You are very special

In all the world there is nobody like you. Since the beginning of time there has never been another person like you. Nobody has your smile, your eyes, your hands, your hair. Nobody owns your handwriting, your voice. YOU'RE SPECIAL.

Nobody can paint your brush strokes. Nobody has your taste for food, or music, or dance, or art. Nobody in the universe sees things as you do. In all time there has never been anyone who laughs in exactly your way, and what makes you laugh or cry or think may have a totally different response in another. So... YOU'RE SPECIAL!

You're different from any other person who has ever lived in the history of the universe. You are the only one in the whole creation who has your particular set of abilities. There is always someone who is better at one thing or another. Every person is my superior in at least one way. Nobody in the universe can reach the quality of the combination of your talents, your feelings. Like a roomful of musical instruments some might excel in one way or another, but nobody can match the symphonic sound when all are played together. YOUR SYMPHONY.

Through all eternity no one will ever walk, talk, think, or do exactly like you. YOU'RE SPECIAL. You are rare and in all rarity there is enormous value and because of your great value the need for you to imitate anyone else is absolutely wrong. YOU ARE SPECIAL and it is no accident you are. Please realise that God made you for a special purpose. He has a job for you to do that nobody else can do as well as you can. Out of billions of applications only one is qualified. Only one has the unique and right combination of what it takes and that one is you. YOU ARE SPECIAL.

November

1 | Spirituality

... My second consideration is aimed particularly to my brother priests... Don't lose sight of your spirituality. The day may come when it's all you've got. When I crumbled and found that I could not move my left leg or my left arm, when I had to be led like a little child, when I didn't know if the next few hours were going to be life or death, all I had was my spiritual peace and my confidence in the Lord. All I could say was, "It is up to you, Lord. I don't know what you are doing to me. I don't like it. I wish you would stop. But whatever it is, I accept. And I accept it for my people's as well as my own sins."

But believe me, my friends, it is all you have. All the rest means nothing. All your strength, all your brains, all your achievements, your honours, your parish – nothing really matters.

You have the Lord and you don't have anything else.

Cardinal G. Emmett Carter
Extract from his Pastoral Letter to the clergy, the religious,
and the faithful people of the Archdiocese of Toronto,
following his stroke on May 29th, 1981

2 | Spirituality

The life of the soul in openess to God,
the waiting,
the periods of aridity,
guilt and despondency,
contrition and repentance, forsakeness,
and hope against hope,
the silent stirrings of love and grace,
trembling on the verge of a certainty

which, if gained, is loss –
the very lightness of this fabric may prove too heavy
    a burden
for men who lust for massively possessive
    experience.

E. Voegelin

3 Spirituality

The day of my spiritual awakening
was the day I saw
– and knew I saw – all things in God
and God in all things.

Mechtild of Magdeburg c. 1210 - 1285

4 Stillness

Sometimes,
    all that God asks of us
    is that
    we sit quietly before him.

Stilling our unconscious need
to be forever doing something for him.

For sometimes,
this yearning to be forever doing
stems not so much from a desire
    to do his Holy Will,
as a desire
to be seen, or to be heard
    in the doing,

and is more
of a projection of our own self-image
seeking the approbation of those whom we know,
rather than God's guidance for us –

Such truths
are never palatable,
and leave a taste of dissatisfaction
which turns sour
as time, and our life's purpose,
    diminishes.

God does not drive us – like slaves and serfs.
It is we who flog ourselves relentlessly on,
and by so doing, destroy that still, small voice
    deep within ourselves.

Work is admirable.
Rest and relaxation are necessary.
But to hear and obey that still, small voice of
our creator –
    that is beyond all else,
    for it is priceless.

Patricia Vardigans

5 Stillness

Only in calm waters can you
see your reflection, not in running
waters. Only in tranquillity
can you find that resting place
which stillness seeks.

Lao-Tse 6th century B.C.

6 | Stillness

Not in the midst of life's tumult nor in the word of pleasure's round does God show himself, but in the inspiration of nature, grace, light as a breath of fresh air in a still small voice.

St Jerome c. 342 - 420

7 | Success

Success is neither fame, wealth nor power;
rather it is seeking, knowing, loving and obeying
    God.
If you seek, you will know;
if you know, you will love;
if you love, you will obey.

Charles Malik

8 | Success

I fear success more than anything. To have succeeded means that one has finished one's work on earth... Life has meaning for me only if it remains a perpetual becoming, a definite goal in front of one and not behind.

George Bernard Shaw 1856 - 1950

9 | Success

Every man who is high up likes to think he has done it all himself, and the wife smiles and lets it go at that.

Sir James M. Barrie 1860 - 1937

10 | Suffering

If my days were untroubled
 and my heart always light
Would I seek that fair land
 where there is no night?
If I never grew weary
 with the weight of my load
Would I search for God's peace
 at the end of the road?
If I never knew sickness
 and never felt pain
Would I reach for a hand
 to help and sustain?
If I walked not with sorrow
 and lived without loss
Would my soul seek sweet solace
 at the foot of the cross?
If all I desired was mine
 day by day
Would I kneel before God
 and earnestly pray?
If God sent no "Winter"
 to freeze me with fear
Would I yearn for the warmth
 of "Spring" every year?
I ask myself this
 and the answer is plain –
If my life were all pleasure
 and I never knew pain
I'd seek God less often
 and need him much less,
For God's sought more often
 in times of distress,
And no one knows God
 or sees him as plain
As those who have met him
 on "The Pathway of Pain".

Indian Inland Mission Bulletin

11 Suffering

He who has suffered most, knows many tongues.
He can be understood, he understands
The language of the countless ones who reach
For sympathy with weak imploring hands...
There will be those who may require of you
Help to go on some first bewildering mile
With grief and pain. God will have need of you
As his interpreter that you may tell
Them of the hope ahead, of the healing years,
And of his love. Oh, learn the language well!

Anon.

12 Suffering

Ah my deare angrie Lord,
Since thou dost love, yet strike:
Cast down, yet help afford;
Sure I will do the like.

I will complain, yet praise
I will bewail, approve,
And all my soure-sweet days
I will lament and love.

Anon. medieval source

13 Suffering

How wonderful it is that literally only Christianity has
taught us the true peace and function of suffering. The
Stoics tried the hopeless little game of denying its
objective reality, or of declaring it as a good in itself
(which it never is), and the Pessimists attempted to

revel in it as a food to their melancholy and as something that can no more be transformed than it can be
avoided or explained. But Christ came and he did not
really explain it. He did far more. He met it, willed it,
transformed it, and he taught us how to do all this, or
rather he himself does it within us, if we do not hinder
his all-healing hands.

Baron Friedrich von Hügel 1852 - 1925
in a letter to a friend in his last illness

14 Suffering

Remember this: All suffering comes to an end. And
whatever you suffer authentically, God has suffered
it first.

Meister Eckhart 1260 - 1329

15 Suffering

Every woman who sees her child,
Every woman who is separated from her child,
Every woman who must stand by helpless
and see her child die,
Every woman who echoes the old cry,
"Why, why, why my child?"
has the answer from the Mother of Christ.
She can look at the child through Mary's eyes,
she can know the answer with Mary's mind,
she can accept the suffering with Mary's will,
she can love Christ in her child with Mary's heart –
because Mary has made her a mother of Christ.
It is Christ who suffers in her child;
it is his innocence redeeming the world,
his love saving the world.

He too is about his Father's business,
the business of love.

Suffering is the price of love.
The hardest thing but the inevitable thing
in the suffering of every individual is that he must
inflict his own suffering on those who love him.

It is love that redeems, love that heals the world,
love that can save.
Suffering has no power in itself;
it is only powerful to save when it is caused by love,
and when it is the expression of love.

Caryll Houselander 1901 - 1954

16 Suffering

Suffering passes,
but the fact of having suffered never leaves us.

Leon Bloy

17 Suffering

God wishes to test you like gold in the furnace. The dross is consumed by the fire, but the pure gold remains and its value increases. It is in this manner that God acts with his good servant, who puts his hope in him and remains unshaken in times of distress. God raises him up, and in return for what he has given up out of love for God, he is repaid a hundredfold in this life and with eternal life hereafter.

St Jerome Emiliani 1481 - 1537

18 | Suffering

Though hard the road you have to tread
   and heavy be the cross –
Though the heart be breaking with a great and
   grievous load ...
Others have travelled ahead of you –
   have groped into the night,
Have struggled through the darkness and come out
   into the light.

The track is marked with footprints where
   unnumbered souls have passed
Through the gates of suffering, and found their
   peace at last ...
Remember this when sorrow comes and when for
   strength you pray:
Others have walked the road before you –
   Others have come this way.

19 | Suffering

Man's extremity is God's opportunity.

John Flavel 1630 - 1691

20 | Suffering

The New Testament teaching on suffering takes it into
an entirely different sphere. Our Lord is not standing by
seeing how we get on, he is actually suffering with us.
Our pain is his pain, our swollen useless limbs are his,
but ultimately our weakness becomes his strength and
our defeat becomes his victory. Here lies one more, and
surely the most profound, truth about suffering: it enables

us to identify more closely with our Lord. Yes, we can
wash each other's feet, we can go about doing good,
on our good days we can show certain Christian virtues. But the Bible speaks of these quite bluntly as
"filthy rags" by contrast with our Lord's perfect life. A
rather sobering thought. But in suffering I believe we
come closest to knowing Christ. Many months before
his actual crucifixion he spoke of his disciples taking
up their cross daily and following him. So I believe suffering prepares us in some special way for our service
in heaven. This may be wishful thinking from one who
has had to endure a great deal, but I believe it to be true.

Dr James H. Casson 1943 - 1980

21 Sympathy

How can anyone sympathise
when sorrow has never put tears in their eyes?
A healing touch never dwelt in the hand that wasn't
by grief taught to understand.
How can a word have the right note of cheer
unless it is bought by experience dear;
and a heart that is broken is better equipped
to mend other hearts that misfortune has chipped.
How can anyone know the cure
unless they themselves have had pain to endure?
Thus when we need comfort where else should we go,
but to one who has passed through the valley of woe.

22 Time

Take time to think –
it is the source of power.
Take time to read –
it is the foundation of wisdom.

Take time to play –
it is the secret of staying young.
Take time to be quiet –
it is the opportunity to seek God.

Take time to be aware –
it is the opportunity to help others.
Take time to love and be loved –
it is God's greatest gift.

Take time to laugh –
it is the music of the soul.
Take time to be friendly –
it is the road to happiness.

Take time to dream –
it is what the future is made of.
Take time to pray –
it is the greatest power on earth.

There is a time for everything...

23 Time

Time is too slow for those who wait,
Too swift for those who fear,
Too long for those who grieve,
Too short for those who rejoice,
But for those who love –
    Time is eternity.

24 Time

It is through the door of the present moment
that God enters into our life,

and it is through you
that he enters into the life of the world.

25 Today

My life is a gift of God,
Given not in years,
    but a day at a time.
Today is the day the Lord has made.
He planned it to be the most important
    day of my life.

Yesterday is gone,
never to return.
I must not worry about it;
but leave it in the hands of God.
Tomorrow and all it holds is God's secret
    and its coming is not assured.

Only today is mine.
Each day arranged by God
    with infinte wisdom and goodness
is his gift, his act of love for me.

In thanksgiving I will offer him
    everyday the gift of myself,
my prayers, works, joys, sufferings.

Dear Lord, graciously receive it.

26 Today

This is the beginning of a new day,
    God has given me this day to use as I will,
        I can waste it or use it for good.

What I do today is important for I am
    exchanging a day of my life for it.
When tomorrow comes this day will be gone
    for ever.
      Leaving in its place something I have traded
        for it.
        I want it to be gain not loss
        good not evil
        success not failure,
In order that I shall not regret
      the price I paid for it.

27 | Today

If we fill our hours with regrets over the failures of
yesterday,
    and with worries over the problems of tomorrow,
      we have no today in which to be thankful.

28 | Tomorrow

The dawn of a new day
means the dawn of a new life –
whatever our yesterdays have been,
tomorrow may be different.
Tomorrow may hold your fate,
tomorrow may mean your victory.
The splendour of the future
lies is the eternal tomorrow,
the day for which
life is worth living.

29 Trials

The gem cannot be polished without friction
   nor man perfected without trials.

Confucius 500 B.C. - 478 B.C.

30 Trinity

We adore you, God the Father, who create us and give
us life; we worship you, Wisdom of the Father, whose
gift of renewed life enables us to live wisely; we praise
you, Holy Spirit, for by loving you, and loving in you,
we live happily and will dwell forever in utmost bliss.
We bless you, three Persons in one God, by whom,
through whom and in whom we exist. Though we turn
from you by sinning and lose our likeness to you, you
continue to uphold us; for you have made us in your
likeness and it is you, the source of life, who renew that
likeness in us. To you be glory for ever and ever. Amen.

William of St-Thierry c. 1085 - 1148

December

1 | Trust

Child of my love, fear not the unknown morrow,
Dread not the new demand life makes of thee.
Thy ignorance doth hold no cause for sorrow
Since what thou knowest not is known to me.

Thou canst not see today the hidden meaning
Of my command, but thou the light shalt gain.
Walk on in faith, upon my promise leaning,
And as thou goest all shall be made plain.

One step thou seest – then go forward boldly,
One step is far enough for faith to see.
Take that, and thy next duty shall be told thee,
For step by step thy Lord is leading thee.

Stand not in fear, thy adversaries counting,
Dare every peril, save to disobey.
Thou shalt march on, all obstacles surmounting,
For I, the Strong, will open up the way.

Wherefore go gladly to the task assigned thee,
Having my promise, needing nothing more
Than just to know, where'er the future find thee,
In all thy journeying I go before.

Frank J. Exeley

2 | Trust

Lead, kindly light, amid the encircling gloom,
Lead thou me on;
The night is dark, and I am far from home,
Lead thou me on.
Keep thou my feet; I do not ask to see
The distant scene; one step enough for me.

I was not ever thus, nor prayed that thou
Shouldst lead me on;
I loved to choose and see my path; but now
Lead thou me on.
I loved the garish day, and spite of fears,
Pride ruled my will: remember not past years.

So long thy power hath blest me, sure it still
Will lead me on
O'er moor and fen, o'er crag and torrent, till
The night is gone,
And with the morn those Angel faces smile,
Which I have loved long since, and lost awhile.

Cardinal John Henry Newman 1801 - 1890

3 | Trust

God only is holy; he alone knows how to lead his children in the paths of holiness. He knows every aspect of your soul, every thought of your heart, every secret of your character, its difficulties and hindrances; he knows how to mould you to his will, and lead you onwards to perfect sanctification; he knows exactly how each event, each trial, each temptation, will tell upon you, and he disposes all things accordingly. The consequences of this belief, if fully grasped, will influence your whole life. You will seek to give yourself up to God more and more unreservedly, asking nothing, refusing nothing, wishing nothing, but what he wills; not seeking to bring things about for yourself, taking all he sends joyfully, and believing the "one step" set before you to be enough for you. You will be satisfied that even though there are clouds around and your way seems dark, he is directing all, and that what seems a hindrance will prove a blessing, since he wills it.

Jean Nicholas Grou SJ 1731 - 1803

4 | Trust

Cast yourself into the arms of God and be very sure that if he wants anything of you, he will fit you for the work and give you strength.

St Philip Neri 1515 - 1595

5 | Trust

God's grace has given the king a gracious frame of mind toward me, so that as yet he has taken from me nothing but my liberty. In doing this His Majesty has done me such great good with respect to spiritual profit that I trust that among all the great benefits he has heaped so abundantly upon me I count my imprisonment the very greatest. I cannot, therefore, mistrust the grace of God.

St Thomas More 1478 - 1535

6 | Trust

Learn to seek God and pray to him regularly during those quiet, mundane times of your life, trusting in his great and infinite loving mercy. Then, when life's storms blow over and around you threatening to engulf you in their ferocity, you can concentrate on what really matters, trusting in your heavenly Father to guide you safely through.

This is the art and secret of prayer – to pray at *all* times, both with thankfulness and praise, trusting in God's heavenly guidance for you, even though all may be dark before you – God has never let anyone down but many have let God down.

7 Trust

My fate is in thy hands,
My God, I wish it there.
My heart my life my health
I leave entirely to thy care.
My fate is in thy hands,
Whatever it may be –
Pleasant or painful, bright or dark –
As best it seems to thee.
My fate is in thy hands,
Why should I doubt or fear.
My Father's heart will never cause
His child a needless tear.

8 Trust

Have courage for the great sorrows of life, and patience
for the small ones. And when you have laboriously
accomplished your daily task, go to sleep in peace.
God is awake.

Victor Hugo 1802 - 1885

9 Trust

How easy it is for me to live with you, Lord!
How easy it is for me to believe in you!
When my mind is distraught and my reason fails,
When the cleverest people do not see further
Than this evening and do not know
What must be done tomorrow,
You grant me the clear confidence
That you exist, and that you will take care
That not all the ways of goodness are stopped.

At the height of earthly fame I gaze
With wonder at that faith through hopelessness
To this point from which
Even I have been able to convey
To men some reflection of the
Light which comes from you.
And you will enable me to go on doing
As much as needs to be done
And in so far as I do not manage it
That means that you have allotted the task to others.

Alexander Solzhenitsyn

10 | Trust

As soon as you turn away – however slightly – from God, and no longer put your trust in him, things go awry; for then the Lord withdraws, as though saying: "You have put your trust in something else – very well, rely on that instead." And whatever it may be, it proves utterly worthless.

Theophan the Recluse

11 | Trust

In pastures green?
Not always; sometimes he
Who knoweth best, in kindness leadeth me
In weary ways where heavy shadows be;
Out of the sunshine, warm and soft and bright,
Out of the sunshine into darkest night,
I oft would faint with sorrow and affright,
Only for this – I know he holds my hand.
So whether in a green or desert land,
I trust him, though I do not understand.

188

And by still waters?
No, not always so;
Oft times the heavy tempests round me blow,
And over my soul the waves and billows go.
But when the storm beats loudest and I cry
Aloud for help, the Master standeth by
And whispers to my soul, "Lo, it is I."
Above the tempest wild I hear him say:
"Beyond this darkness lies the perfect day,
In every path of thine I lead the way."

So, whether on the hilltop high and fair
I dwell, or in the sunless valley where
The shadows lie – what matter? He is there.
Yea, more than this, where'er the pathway lead,
He gives to me no helpless, broken reed,
But his own hand sufficient for my need.
So where'er he leadeth I can safely go;
And in the blest hereafter I shall know
Why, in his Wisdom; he hath led me so.

Anon.

12 | Unity

Lord Jesus, who on the eve of your death prayed that
all your disciples might be one, as you are in the Father
and the Father in you, make us feel intense sorrow over
the infidelity of our disunity. Give us the honesty to
recognise, and the courage to reject, whatever differences towards one another or mutual distrust or even
enmity lie hidden within us. Enable all of us to meet
one another in you. And let our prayers for the unity of
Christians be ever in our hearts and on our lips – unity
such as you desire it and by the means that you will.
Make us find the way that leads to unity, in you who
are perfect charity, through being obedient to the Spirit
of love and truth. Amen.

Shankill and Falls Clergy Fellowship, Belfast

189

13 Unity

Lord of all creation,
we stand in awe before you,
impelled by visions of the harmony of man.
We are children of many traditions –
inheritors of shared wisdom
and tragic misunderstandings,
of proud hopes and humble successes.
Now it is time for us to meet –
in memory and truth,
in courage and trust,
in love and promise.

In that which we share,
let us see the common prayer of humanity;
in that in which we differ,
let us wonder at the freedom of man;
in our unity and our differences,
let us know the uniqueness that is God.

Forms of prayer for Jewish people

14 Unity

Grant, O merciful Lord, to all pastors,
in whatever communion they be,
such a spirit that they may daily lament
the divisions of Christendom,
and express a common zeal for healing them.
Let this spirit be such as was given
to the Apostles –
not of fierceness and passion,
but of meekness.
May the same heavenly light attend them
to discover to them the things
that are for peace,

and in this disposition,
may they unite their labours
and have thy blessing
for bringing all to good effect.

O God, how glorious would Sion be
were all united in one faith.

Fr John Gother ? - 1704

15 Weakness

Lord,
In the weakness that has overcome me,
I cry to you for help.
You took our weakness on yourself when you
suffered and died for us.
You share our weakness now
as though it were your own,
so that it may have some purpose and value.
I cannot understand this myself;
but trusting in you I surrender my weakness,
my pain, my sickness, my fears to you.
Help me to bear this ungrudgingly
and to offer this generously through you
to the Father of mercies who awaits
us all with the gift of eternal life.
Amen.

Bishop Francis Thomas 1930 - 1988

16 Will of God

It is in choosing to serve God, to do his will, that man
achieves his highest and fullest freedom. It may seem
paradoxical to say that our highest and fullest freedom

comes when we follow to the least detail the will of another, but it is true nonetheless when that other is God. I could testify from my own experiences, especially from my darkest hours in Lubianka, that the greatest sense of freedom, along with peace of soul and an abiding sense of security, comes when a man totally abandons his own will in order to follow the will of God. Never again could I doubt that the greatest assurance I could have in my life came from knowingly and willingly following God's will as manifested to me. I knew only too well how shallow and unsafe it was for me to follow my own will, my own inclinations and desires, unless they were in conformity to his. I realized then, and I felt it more deeply each day, that true freedom meant nothing else than letting God operate within my soul without interference, giving preference to God's will as manifested in the promptings, inspirations, and other means he chose to communicate, rather than in acting on my own initiatives.

Walter J. Ciszek SJ

17 | Will of God

Your life is a quiet round of common and homely things. You dream perhaps of a wider sphere, and sigh for a great and useful life. You question whether it is right that life should be such a miserable bundle of very little things. But nothing is little that is done for God, and it must be right if it be his will. If this common life with its homely things is God's discipline for you, be assured that in your small corner, unobserved, unambitious, your lot is very near, very dear to God.

18 | Will of God

The life of the world goes on through the will of some one. Some one makes our own life and that of the universe his own inscrutable care. To have a hope of understanding what that will means, we must first carry it out, we must do what is required of us. Unless I do what is required of me, I can never know what that may be, and much less know what is required of us all and of the whole universe.

Leo Tolstoy 1828 - 1910

19 | Will of God

Only one thing is important, whether we are brave or cowardly: to be always there where God will have us, and for the rest to trust him. There is no other remedy against fear but to abandon ourselves to his will.

Georges Bernanos 1888 - 1948

20 | Wisdom

We learn wisdom from failure more than from success. We often discover what will do, by finding out what will not do. Great thoughts, discoveries, inventions have very generally been nurtured in hardship, often pondered over in sorrow and established with difficulty.

Paxton Hood

21 | Wisdom

Wisdom (i.e., holiness) consists in doing the next thing you have to do, doing it with your whole heart, and finding delight in doing it.

Meister Eckhart 1260 - 1329

22 | Witness

No witness reaches our contemporaries more persuasively than the witness of Christians who do what Jesus did.

Anthony Padovano

23 | Worry

Philosophy from the trenches – First World War

When you are a soldier you are one of two things, either at the front or behind the lines. If you are behind the lines you need not worry. If you are at the front you are one of two things. You are either in a danger zone or in a zone which is not dangerous. If you are in a zone which is not dangerous you need not worry. If you are in a danger zone you are one of two things: either you are wounded, or you are not. If you are not wounded you need not worry. If you are wounded you are one of two things: either seriously wounded or slightly wounded. If you are slightly wounded you need not worry. If you are seriously wounded, one of two things is certain: either you will get well or you will die. If you get well, you needn't worry. If you die, you cannot worry. So there is no need to worry about anything at all.

Quoted by Vera Brittain 1896 - 1970
in The Testament of Youth

24 | Worry

I have nothing to do with tomorrow,
My Saviour will make that his care;
Should he fill it with trouble and sorrow
He'll help me to suffer and bear.
I have nothing to do with tomorrow.
Its burdens then why should I share?
Its grace and its faith I can't borrow.
Then why should I borrow its care?

25 | December 25th

The Lord of all comes in the form of a servant; and he comes as a poor man, so that he will not frighten away those souls he seeks to capture like a huntsman. He is born in an obscure town, deliberately choosing a humble dwelling-place. His mother is a simple maiden, not a great lady. And the reason for all this lowly state is so that he may gently ensnare mankind and bring us to salvation.

If he had been born amid the splendour of a rich family, unbelievers would surely have said that the face of the world had been changed by the power of wealth. If he had chosen to be born in Rome, the greatest of cities, they would have ascribed the same change to the power of her citizens.

Suppose our Lord had been the son of an emperor; they would have pointed to the advantage of authority. Imagine his father a legislator; their cry would have been, "See what can be brought about by the law". But, in fact, what did he do? He chose nothing but poverty and mean surroundings, everything that was plain and ordinary and, in the eyes of most people, obscure. And this so that it could be clearly seen that the Godhead alone transformed the world. That was why he chose his mother from among the poor of a very poor country, and became poor himself.

This is the lesson of the crib. Since there was no bed, our Lord was laid in a manger. This lack of the necessities of life was the best way of proclaiming the will of God. He was laid in a manger to show that he was to be the food even of simple folk. We know, in fact, how the divine Word, the Son of God, drew to himself both rich and poor, the eloquent and the inarticulate, as he lay in the manger surrounded by poverty.

See then how poverty acted as a prophecy – how his poverty showed that he who became poor for our sake is thereby made accessible to everyone. Christ made no ostentatious display of riches, which would have made people frightened to approach him; he assumed no royal state, which would have driven men away from his presence. No, he came among ordinary men as one of themselves, offering himself freely for the salvation of all mankind.

Theodotus ? - 445

26 Worry

Worry does not empty
tomorrow of its sorrow;
    it empties today of its strength.
It does not enable us to escape evil;
    it makes us unfit to face evil when it comes;
it is the interest you pay on trouble before it comes.

27 | Worry

The crosses which we make for ourselves,
   by a restless anxiety as to the future,
are not crosses which come from God.

Anon.

28 | Worry

I am an old man and have known a great many troubles, but most of them have never happened.

Mark Twain 1830 - 1910

29 | Youth

He was so young

He was so young, God.

So young and strong and filled with promise. So vital, so radiant, giving so much joy wherever he went.

He was so brilliant. On this one boy you lavished so many talents that could have enriched your world. He had already received so many honours, and there were so many honours to come.

Why then? In our agony we ask, Why him? Why not someone less gifted? Someone less good? Some rioter, thief, brute?

Yet we know, even as we demand what seems to us a rational answer, that we are only intensifying our grief. Plunging deeper into the blind and witless place where all hope is gone. A dark lost place where our own gifts will be blunted and ruin replace the goodness he brought and wished for us.

Instead let us thank you for the marvel that this boy was. That we can say goodbye to him without shame or regret, rejoicing in the blessed years he was given to us. Knowing that his bright young life, his many gifts, have not truly been stilled or wasted, only lifted to a higher level where the rest of us can't follow yet.

Separation? Yes. Loss? Never.

For his spirit will be with us always. And when we meet him again we will be even more proud.

Thank you for this answer, God.

Marjorie Holmes

30 Zeal

Whenever we find ourselves more inclined to persecute than to persuade, we may then be certain that our zeal has more of pride in it than of charity.

Charles Caleb Colton 1780 - 1832

31 December 31st

God be with you in the dying of the year and at its birth; in the ending of a page of your life and your work, in the turning of another, with all that it may bring back.

God be with your heart, that it may love what he loves: that you may love the things of earth as he has ordained. No more, no less: that your love be wise, loyal and generous, forgiving and understanding: not demanding too much, nor giving too little; that you may have strength to face the future; to leave it in his hands, patient in sorrow: grateful in joy.

God be with your speech, that you may not wound the heart of any man, may not affront his dignity nor lessen your own: that your words may lighten and console, may lift up the hearts of others to laughter, shining through their tears, to peace in the midst of storm, to light in darkness.

God be in your eyes, that you may see clearly and cleanly, that you may see beyond the small and mean, the things that matter and the broad road of your duty and your work in life, and not be drawn away by petty paths: that you may see your neighbour's needs and not his faults: his striving and goodwill and not his human failings.

God be with your hands, to heal and not to hurt: to build and not to spoil, to work and not to be idle.

God be with you, that you may not shirk the paths of mercy nor weary in the succouring of any neighbour's need.

God be with you in your home and give you there the precious things that matter more than all the world: love, service, and unswerving loyalty, peace and a common understanding that no power on earth or hell may undermine.

God shower you with graces, aid you with his saints, guard you with his angels, bless you with the blessings of Mary the Queen, Virgin and Mother, that hand in hand with Christ, her Son, you may walk securely through all your ways, now and always.

Caryll Houselander 1901 - 1954

Index of authors

Adam of Perseigne: *Love*
Aelred of Rievaulx, St:
  Friendship
Albion, Canon Gordon:
  Others
Allen, Woody: *Death*
Amiel, Henri-Frederic: *Old
  age*
Andrew, Fr.: *Friendship*
Anselm, St: *Gratitude*
Anthony, Mary Claret, St:
  Cross the, Holiness
Appleton, George: *Peace*
Arias, Juan: *God*
Armstrong, Elodie:
  Commandments
Augustine, St: *Searching*
Aumonier, Minnie: *God*

Baker, Josephine: *Old age*
Bekr, Abu: *Prayer*
Barclay, William:
  Friendship, Holiness
Barrie, Sir James M.:
  Success
Basil, St: *Comfort*
Bernanos, Georges: *Will of
  God*
Bernard of Clairvaux, St:
  Mary
Bierce, Ambrose: *Christian*
Binyon, Laurence:
  Remembrance
Blake, William: *Sorrow*
Bloy, Leon: *Suffering*
Bonhoeffer, Dietrich:
  Morning Prayer
Boon, Bernard: *Generosity*
Bosco, St John: *Gentleness,
  Reconciliation*

Bossuet, Jacques: *Adoration*
Boyd, Major Malcolm:
  Death
Brittain, Vera: *Worry*
Brown, David: *Potential*
Bryant, Sir Arthur: *Giving*
Buffett, Gerald: *Purpose*
Butler, Bishop Christopher:
  Sinners

Cabodovilla, J.M.: *Prayer*
Camara, Archbishop Helder
  Holiness
Carrel, Alexis: *Prayer*
Carretto, Carlo: *Forgiveness*
Carter, Cardinal G. Emmett:
  Spirituality
Casaroli, Cardinal Agostino:
  Dialogue
Cassiodorus: *God*
Casson, James H.: *Hope,
  Suffering*
Chandler, Bishop Arthur:
  Disillusionment
Chantry, June: *Easter*
Chautard: *God*
Chrysostom, St John:
  Preaching
Cicero: *Grief*
Ciszek, Walter J.: *Will of
  God*
Cleeve, R.E.: *Commendation*
Cockett, Michael: *Jesus
  Christ*
Coleridge, Samuel Taylor:
  The Bible
Colton, Charles Caleb: *Zeal*
Confucius: *Trials*
Cookson, Catherine: *Silence*
Cuhel, Lois Mae: *Self*

201

Sources and Acknowledgements

Permission to reproduce copyright material in this book is gratefully acknowledged:

"Belief", Katie Jackson (Outposts Publications, 1979); "Christianity" © Fr Donal Spring; "Compassion", Jean Vanier (Darton, Longman & Todd); "Death", Marjorie Holmes, *Who Am I Speaking to God?* © 1969 (Doubleday & Co, New York); "Death", Michael Hollings and Etta Gullick, *The Shade of His Hand* (Mayhew-McCrimmon 1973); "Death", Thomas Merton, *Conjectures of a Guilty Bystander* (Abbey of Gethsemani); "Hope", James Casson, *Dying - the Greatest Adventure of my Life* (Christian Medical Fellowship); "Easter" © June Chantry; "Easter", Flor McCarthy (Dominican Publications); "Failure", Robert Llewelyn, *The Joy of the Saints* (Darton, Longman & Todd); "Fear": Dame Cicely Saunders for permission to use Sidney Reeman's poem; "Forgiveness" © Patricia Vardigans; "Forgiveness", Carlo Carretto, *In Search of Beyond* (Darton, Longman & Todd); "Forgiveness", Paul Tournier, *The Person Reborn* (SCM Press); "Generosity" © Bernard Boon; "God" © Robina Knewstub; "God's plan", John Main OSB, *The Joy of Being* (Darton, Longman & Todd and the executors of John Main OSB); "Handicapped" © Patricia Davis; "Help Unfailing" © Frank Topping (Lutterworth Press); "Holiness", William Barclay, *Prayers for the Christian Year* (SCM Press 1974); "Holy Spirit", Prayer of a Young Ghanaian Christian, from *Morning, Noon and Night*, edited by the Rev. John Carden (The Church Missionary Society 1976); "Individuality" © Patricia Vardigans; "Jesus Christ", Paul Tournier, *To Resist or to Surrender?* (SCM Press); "Jesus Christ" © Michael Cockett; "Life", Eric Doyle OFM, *St Francis and the Song of Brotherhood* (Franciscan Community, Canterbury); "Love", Bishop Richard Harries, *Prayer and the Pursuit of Happiness* (Fount 1985); "Love", William Rees-Mogg, *An Humbler Heaven* (Hamish Hamilton 1977); "Meditation", John Main OSB, *The Joy of Being* (Darton, Longman & Todd and the executors of John Main OSB); "Nurse"s Prayer", Alwyn M. Law, (*This England* magazine, Autumn 1988); "Peace", George Appleton, *Jerusalem Prayers for the World Today* (SPCK 1974); "Potential" © David Brown; "Poverty", Flor McCarthy (Dominican Publications); "Prayer" © C.M. Ford; "Prayer", James Roose-Evans, *Inner Journey, Outer Journey* (David Highams Associated Ltd); "Prayer", John Dalrymple, *Costing not less than everything* (Darton, Longman & Todd); "Prayer", *Forms of Prayer for Jewish Worship* (The Reform Synagogues of Great Britain 1978); "Religious Experience", Paul Tournier, *The Strong and the Weak* (SCM Press 1963); "Sickness" © C.M. Ford; "Silence" © Winifred M.

Eddison; "Silence" © 1988 Catherine Cookson, extracted from *Let me Make Myself Plain* (Bantam Press. All rights reserved); "Reconciliation, Litany of", first published in *Sharing the Pain - Pastoral Guidelines* by Bill Kirkpatrick (Darton, Longman & Todd); "Solitude", Jean Vanier, *Community and Growth* (Darton, Longman & Todd); "Spirituality" by Cardinal Gerald Emmett Carter; "Stillness" © Patricia Vardigans; "Suffering", James Casson, *Dying - the Greatest Adventure of my Life* (Christian Medical Fellowship); "Timelessness", George Appleton (SPCK); "Unity", from *Daily, Sabbath and Occasional Prayers* (Reform Synagogues of Great Britain 1977); "Will of God", Walter J. Ciszek SJ, *He Leadeth Me* (Hodder & Stoughton).

Every effort has been made to ensure the accuracy of copyright acknowledgements. The compiler and publishers of this book apologise for any inadvertent omissions of copyright and will rectify this in future editions where such omissions or infringements are brought to their attention.

By the same author:

WORDS OF WISDOM

"Father Danny Cronin has brought together in this book an interesting collection of thoughts, one for each day. People today often find that they do not have time for reading spiritual books, others are not accustomed to the practice of spiritual reading. This book will help those who want something brief, and it may be an encouragement to others to read books that feed our faith.

There is much in this book to feed the spirit. It is hoped that it will prompt and inspire quiet meditation and fervent prayer."

(*Cardinal Basil Hume*, in the Preface)

ISBN 085439 284 X

WORDS OF ENCOURAGEMENT

An extremely varied and balanced collection of thoughts from different times, places and cultures. A quotation is alloted to each day of the year according to a system of themes. In a world where, along with its beauty and goodness, there is much pain and suffering, readers will find in this book eloquent words of encouragement from many people in different circumstances.

ISBN 085439 422 2